Chapman

Irish Issue: 'Fla...

KV-578-166

ISBN 0 906772 88 5   ISSN 0308-2695   © *Chapman* 1999

CHAPMAN

4 Broughton Place, Edinburgh EH1 3RX, Scotland
E-mail: chapman_pub@ndirect.co.uk
Website: www.airstrip-one.ndirect.co.uk/chapman
Tel 0131–557 2207 Fax 0131–556 9565

Editor: Joy Hendry   **Assistant Editor: Gerry Stewart**
Guest Editor: Hayden Murphy

*Volunteers: Valerie Brotherton, Marie Carter, Becky England, Gary Flockhart, Pat Fox,
Colin Mackay and Emma Pitcairn.*

Submissions:
*Chapman welcomes submissions of poetry,
fiction and articles provided they are
accompanied by a stamped addressed
envelope or International Reply Coupons*

Subscriptions:

	Personal		Institutional	
	1 year	2 years	1 year	2 years
UK	£16	£30	£20	£38
Overseas	£21/$35	£39/$65	£25/$43	£47$75

THE SCOTTISH **ARTS** COUNCIL

Printed by Inglis Allen, Middlefield Road, Falkirk FK2 9AG

Acknowledgements

Thanks to *Chapman* for the invitation to edit the first Irish issue for 21 years, since *Chapman 19*: 1977. Also to all contributors both invited and submitting. The final selection is mine.

Particular thanks to poet Thomas Kinsella for permission to publish his *Preface on Peppercanister 1972-1997*. It first appeared in the *Archives and Libraries Series*, No 3, 1997 of Emory University, USA (compiler Stephen Enniss).

A nod of friendship to artist John Behan for taking time when preparing for a London Irish Embassy exhibition to do the special cover and front-piece.

An acknowledgement of receipt, from Harry Gilonis, of the text *For the Birds*, poems collated for *Cork Conference Proceedings*. As a separate entity in this issue they were outside my editorial remit. I recommend them to other editors interested in Irish writing.

Finally may I welcome the first Irish Consul to Scotland, Dan Mulhall, and thank him for agreeing to preface the Gael-force that opens these pages.

This Irish Issue is dedicated to the memory of Lar Cassidy (18 June 1950 - 8 October 1997). Literature Officer in the Irish Arts Council (since 1980), Assistant Register of *Aos Dana* (from 1983). He was, in his final year, Director of *Ireland and its Diaspora* at the 1996 Frankfurt Book Fair. He is a friend. Death cannot diminish that. As Seamus Heaney said at the Glasnevin Crematorium "Lar had virtue, in the root sense of the word – he had pure worth and strength as a *vir*, a man. He had valour, principle, and the force of being that comes from principle . . . he had what Aristotle called magnificence".

Cover: John Behan RHA: *Flames of History* after John F Deane's 'The Dead and the Undead of St Michan's'

Frontpiece: John Behan: *McGinty's Goat*

Illustration by John Behan

Preface

Daniel Mulhall, Consul General of Ireland

When the Taoiseach, Bertie Ahern, delivered the Lothian Lecture in Edinburgh in October 1998 under the evocative title, 'The Western Isles of Europe at the Millennium', he spoke of the potential for a challenging new relationship between Ireland and Scotland, primed by our deep historical connections as well as by more recent developments in our two countries and in the wider European context. When I learned of Hayden Murphy's plans to bring a collection of contemporary Irish writing to a Scottish audience, it struck me that this initiative was nicely in tune with the broader economic and political parameters sketched by the Taoiseach.

The Good Friday Agreement, with its provision for a new British-Irish Council, and the onset of the Scottish devolution, offers great scope for the Irish and the Scots to add new strands to the already rich texture of our traditional ties. This will allow fresh voices of dialogue to make themselves heard. There are many ways in which today's Ireland can address today's Scotland, but literature is an obvious medium of interaction. English, Gaelic and Scots afford a varied linguistic environment in which to carry messages back and forth across the narrow stretch of sea that flows between us.

Many of the same Irish and Scottish writers already have readerships in both countries. I recently came across a striking expression of this reality. The words of the Robert Burns poem, 'The Tree of Liberty' are chiselled into the footpath at the site of the monument in Wexford Town to the rising of 1798, while a nearby plaque recognises Scottish 'New Light' Presbyterianism, alongside the American and French Revolutions, as one of the inspirational roots of the rebellion.

This Irish issue of *Chapman* provides a link between a distinguished group of Irish writers and their Scottish readers. It gives a flavour of the strength and diversity of contemporary Irish writing. There is a special value in assembling a collection of this kind. It will enable Scottish readers (as well as *Chapman* readers further afield) who are familiar with individual Irish writers to revisit them through new works appearing alongside pieces by writers they may not have encountered before. The breadth and quality of this collection testify to the editor's outstanding commitment to nurturing cultural connections between Ireland and Scotland.

Introduction: Editorial

Thank you Mrs Robinson for Putting our Writers on your Stage

Hayden Murphy

To frame a literary Irish Issue around an Irish political career may seem perverse, faction opening in fact. I will not justify it by my own personal admiration and approval of my former Trinity College colleague President Mary Robinson (Bourke). I will though take 1991-97 as a period when a President engaged with a pride of poets informed by a 'rainbow collection' of views and attitudes.

The image of President Robinson, hand in hand with the poet Seamus Heaney, waltzing down the corridors of Aras an Uactarain, celebrating his Nobel laureateship in 1995 is an iconic memory. She now works for peace and reconciliation in the UN. 1998 can be celebrated as a year when Peace broke out in Ireland. As a direct result Scotland welcomed its first Consul General from Ireland. His first official exercise was to write the Preface for this issue. Poetry becomes Peace's advocate.

In a beautiful farewell to her friend, our President, Eavan Boland (*Irish Times*, March 15, 1997) spoke of empathy with affection. Then the Dubliner disclosed that the Mayo-born First Lady, who launched her campaign in Kerry, and pointedly included Belfast in her Presidential itinerary, loved to quote Yeats's all embracing phrase from his essay 'The Galway Plains'. He was speaking of community. "There is still in truth upon these level plains a people, a community bound together by imaginative possessions."

At Number One St Columbs Street, Edinburgh, in September 1998 Ireland opened its first ever Consulate to Scotland. A direct result of the Good Friday Agreement. Colum Cille (?521-597) left Ireland after losing a court case over the ownership of a copy he made, without permission, of the Psalter of St Finnian of Moville. Sentenced to exile he sailed with 12 others to Iona to found a monastery and die. Literature can be the making and breaking of reputations.

In October 1998 John Hume (with David Trimble) was awarded the Nobel Peace Prize. Like Heaney he went to St Columb's school in Derry. Coincidences are great introductions to contracting editorials.

> Perhaps the English Committees . . . would never have sent you my name if I had written no plays, no dramatic criticism, if my lyric poetry had not a quality of speech practised upon the stage, perhaps even – though this could be no portion of their deliberate thought – if it were not in some degree the symbol of a movement. – Yeats: Nobel Acceptance Lecture, 1923.

Mnemonic for an Imagination:

Laid back to back the memories elide.

Mid-March 1977, post St Patrick's Day. H is in Edinburgh. Chapman *summons. In Duddingston Park Tom Scott waves him in. Kirsty, the dog, blinks at being stepped over. Joy takes over the texts for* Chapman 19. *Twenty-*

6

one years later H twitches on Broughton Street. Copy for Chapman 92 is late. The survivors over the decades in the two Irish Issues are Brendan Kennelly, Hugh Maxton, Hayden Murphy and Desmond O'Grady.

Memory regresses. Dublin 1968. Neary's Bar. Duffle-coated doubles. Seamus Heaney, wary from the North, meets H for the first time, and then John Behan. From there poems, visual interpretations and Broadsheet (1967-78) leads to resurrections and retrospectives in Edinburgh in 1983.

> Illusions fall away one after another like
> the husks of a fruit, and that fruit is experience. – Gerard de Nerval

It is 1974. H, returning from Barcelona, pauses in London. He listens to the wisdom of years from Timothy O'Keeffe. The publisher who brought Patrick Kavanagh, sustained Hugh MacDiarmid, and maintained Francis Stuart for British readers. Broadsheet is in flux. Advice is welcomed.

A literary magazine needs editorial unity and eccentricity from its contributors. Avoid themes. They slow your imagination down. Whisper in editorials, shouts and clamours distract from contributions's content and contributors' consent. Enjoy measuring out opinions but leave judgements to the reader. Always listen to the established but be willing to hear the new. But always have your own sense of unity.

Reclaiming the past. It is 1965. Trinity College, Dublin, undergraduate H is 'Presidential Election Agent' for the 'non-party aligned' Eoin O'Mahony. 'The Pope'. So called for his infallible self-belief. H gets constitutional advice from Mary Bourke of the Law Society. On a social occasion in the following year Fabian H dances, nose to navel, with his advisor, grateful that 'The Pope' failed by two votes to scrape on to the nomination papers. De Valera is returned. Big Fellow back in Big House.

Mid-1990. H, after decades of non-political alignment, works from abroad in the Presidential campaign of one Mary Robinson. Part of a rainbow coalition of parties and pieties. Clowns, literally of the circus sort, to Communists. Platitudes of cross-party politicians and an Aos Dana of artists. In her inauguration speech she quotes poets (see Chapman 69-70: Autumn 1992). The Big House is enlarged by echoes.

Exile. It has nothing to do with place. As Joyce has written: "I have lived so long abroad and in so many countries that I can feel at once the voice of Ireland in anything".

A place that ever was lived in is like a fire that never goes out. It flares up, it smoulders for a time, it is fanned or smothered by circumstances, but its being is intact, forever fluttering within it, the result of some original ignition. Sometimes its little light must be sought out to be seen, small and tender as a candle flame, but as certain. – Eudora Welty: *Some Notes on River Country* (1944).

Exile. It has all to do with absences. Early 1975 H is in Berlin. Beckett is directing Waiting for Godot. "If this doesn't purge them, then nothing will." Friend Awe competes with enemy Earnestness. In the Schiller-Theatre words go on. Lucky's speech is being discussed. Anxious actor: "Belcher, the Navigator?" Beckett: "No, no, Belcher, that is the opposite of Fartov. English to fart. Belcher to belch". At home at last when the false mystique of Beckett disrobes.

It is back to 1971. H and Trevor Royle overview Sorley MacLean speak of James Connelly in Trinity College's Common Room. Spacious words resonate. Dragged from McDaid's pub Christy and Mattie O'Neill, IRA internees in the Curragh during the war, weep for pacifism. H's self-adopted foster-father Liam Brady holding his hand. Bloomsday looms. Then the heartstops in January 1972 on the streets of Derry. H has started to move away.

In a Dublin ruin of a church, beside water, flames of history lie. Total recall is often false memory.

I am in fact straining towards a strain . . .

I also strain towards this in the poetry I read. And I find it, for example, in the repetition of that refrain of Yeats's "Come build in the empty house of the stare", with its tone of supplication, its pivots of strength in the words 'build' and 'house' and its acknowledgement of dissolution in the word 'empty'. I find it also in the triangle of forces held in equilibrium by the triple rhyme of 'fantasies' and 'enmities' and 'honey-bees', and in the sheer in-placeness of the whole poem as a given form within the language. Poetic form is both the ship and the anchor. It is at once a buoyancy and a holding, allowing for the simultaneous gratification of whatever is centrifugal and centripetal in mind and body. And it is by such means that Yeats's work does what the necessary poetry always does, which is to touch the base of our unsympathetic reality of the world in to which that nature is constantly exposed. The form of the poem in other words, is crucial to poetry's power to do the thing which always is and always will be to poetry's credit: the power to persuade that vulnerable part of our consciousness of its rightness in spite of the evidence of wrongness all around it, the power to remind us that we are hunters and gathers of values, that our very solitudes and distresses are creditable, in so far as they, too, are an earnest of our veritable human being. – Heaney: Nobel Acceptance Lecture, 1995.

Finally a note on how this issue was compiled. It has had a year to grow. Primarily I decided for reasons of length and commerce to focus on poetry though welcoming fiction and drama publications for the review section.

First I contacted twenty-two writers on a personal basis for contributions. Sixteen were willing and able to submit new work. Then, through the *Poetry Ireland Newsletter* I threw out an open invitation for contributions. The response was immediate and stimulating. Finally I used *The Irish Times* 'Bookworm' column (compiler John Boland) to alert publishers to the issue and maybe further poets. Postmen ached.

From over three hundred submissions the subsequent entries are due solely to my editing, my choices. In the review sections I diversified. The duality of playwright/performer dictated Drama. Yeats's *The Circus Animals' Desertion* gave me lines to frame new fictions (and yes I *do* know I cheated on chronology!). There are 18 paragraphs on poetry. Who knows, but me, it may be a nod towards *Ulysses*. The short introduction to Irish publishing is but a brief.

It is 21 years since I have shuffled opinions with judgements. This is my final editorial.

Peppercanister, 1972-97: Twenty-five Years of Poetry

Thomas Kinsella

Peppercanister was established in 1972 as a small publishing enterprise, issuing occasional special items from our home in Dublin, across the Grand Canal from St Stephen's Church, known familiarly as 'The Peppercanister'.

The idea originated with *Butcher's Dozen*, written in April 1972 in response to the Widgery Report on the 'Bloody Sunday' shootings in Derry. The poem was finished quickly and issued as a simple pamphlet at ten pence a copy; cheapness and coarseness were part of the effect, as with a ballad sheet. I thought at first of keeping the poem anonymous and using 'Peppercanister' in place of a name, but when the time came I felt it better to sign the poem. Peppercanister was kept as a personal mark. The Dolmen Press was not involved with *Butcher's Dozen*, but Liam Miller was personally interested and helped with practical suggestions.

A Selected Life was issued as a commemorative elegy, with *Butcher's Dozen* as a precedent but using better materials, and designed by Liam Miller for the serious occasion. *Vertical Man* was issued a year later as a sequel in the same format. The fourth title, *The Good Fight*, was issued as a small public pamphlet with some of the character of *Butcher's Dozen*.

It seemed that Peppercanister was developing as a means of dealing with occasional public items. But the next titles were different, in content and purpose. *One* and *A Technical Supplement* were closer to book-length and contained sequences of a more private poetry. Used in this way, for sequences and short collections, Peppercanister became an alternative to the publication of poetry in literary journals. I had always found this unsatisfactory, with the poems placed between stories and articles and disappearing with a particular issue. Later Peppercanister sequences and short collections were *Song of the Night and Other Poems*, *Songs of the Psyche*, *Personal Places*, *Poems from Centre City* and *Madonna*.

The idea proved useful also for the separate publication of long poems: *The Messenger*, *Her Vertical Smile*, *Out of Ireland* and *St Catherine's Clock*; and including two satirical poems: *One Fond Embrace* and *Open Court*.

Most of the Peppercanister titles were issued with special editions, on handmade paper, boxed, and with full leather bindings. I had admired Liam Miller's commitment to quality in materials and design, and for a while this was confused with the Peppercanister idea. But the production and distribution of special editions is a special matter, and Peppercanister as it has developed is useful above all as a form of interim publication, providing an extra draft of the text, in book form, before final publication.

Current Peppercanister editions, from *One Fond Embrace* (1988) to *The Pen Shop* (1997), are produced and distributed by Dedalus Press as individually designed small books, without specials, making use of 'Peppercanister' as a personal mark. *The Dual Tradition,* a long prose essay on poetry and politics in Ireland, was published in 1995 by Carcanet Press, also with the Peppercanister mark; this is distributed in Ireland by Dedalus Press.

Future plans are for the continued interim publication of poetry; with prose essays, including the detailed reading and evaluation of individual poems from the tradition and by contemporary poets.

Desmond O'Grady

Halloween

for Patrick and Ursula Creagh

Halloween weekend and this year's harvest
of life and death. We escape our city world
for the country and your autumnal farmhouse.
Honest joy of friends' visit to friends for old
times' sake. Glasses of welcome. Sit to the feast.
Eat and drink well with toasts to past and future,
then settle round the open fire in three generations.

Now disguised, our scarum children play games,
dare each other to poke frightened fingers at shadows
on walls in Find the Fairy. The grandmother evokes
old times, ghosts and games of her own childhood.
We muse round, the cauldron hangs on the flames,
share hopes and fears of the magic that outside
brews for the growing generation around us.

The fire burns down. The dog outside howls
at the moon for entrance. Lanterns reflect thoughts
of dead friends in our last glass of hot punch.
It's time to throw salt in corners, ashes and water
out on the dead land, place cross on door, light candle.

Corncobs decorate our bedposts. "Good night.
Don't let old ghosts fright. Hold your fernseed tight."

Grandson

You open your day, our lives, as the lead actor
his theatre. Welcomed, you're prepared for today's
performance with women's talk. Disrobe. Pose with pleasure,
then don the costume tailored for your new play's
old story and stroll out on your stage that reflects our world.
We play to your gestures, plain or purled.

Your first act's set in spring green garden sunshine
where you delight in the morning's comedy with reclined
waves, held gasps, small smiles. Your orchestration.
The players in your park respond in kind.
A pal, or dog you grant men's talk attention,
but your sight's set on grander satisfaction.

Lunch, like newspapers, serves prescribed plates of talk,
that three course play within the play. You sit

up to and hold the table with each remark.
Eat well, then have something to show for it.
Afternoon, like history, gives pause for reflection
on life's confusion and its safe solution.
Nightfall. Your bath is drawn after you dine
so you may wash away your day's distractions.
Then you both plot. She with her glass of wine,
you with your bottle, like two gay tragedians.
Darkness beds you. Sound sleep brings on those dreams,
nightmares that act out your still small boy's schemes.

Odyssey

Light off the Atlantic again on my hometown in autumn
and the familiar expanse of our island's Ocean. I'm back
from Tabriz and those Maikop horsetamers on Azerbijan's
plateau. My idealistic journey there. 'Go to the source of
your race's origin', thought I. 'Follow those various trails
taken by the original wandering Celts. Return through time
by that route that leads from the Caspian Sea to Connemara.
That one's more ethnic than the Amber Route you traversed.'

I went. Now home again I know, from so real an experience,
why my people emigrated from there so long ago; not from my
youthfully imagining it all in school and library reading.
Was it Milton who proposed we should first study in books
who we are, then travel to witness the reality in person?
I believe we should. Returned we can tell our story to others.

Eithne Strong

An Pháirc Fíogadán

I ndeireadh na dáia
cad is fiú
sainmhíniú?

Tá ann fós Sernobil,
an Meánoirthear, 'próiséis shíochána',
na milliúin faoi dhaorsmacht, ghorta . . .
an domhan mailaithe.

Glac do rogha –
Búda, Críost, Mahomet,
nó córas nár leo:
fiúntas anseo, ansiúd ach . . .

Túr Bháibil ba chruinn mar shiombal –
círéib gan sárú, an fhís ina fál
nár dreapadh fós.

Scrios, díothú, fuath:
más máthair is ciontach.
Ar teitheadh atáimse –
on gcíréib lastigh.

Ní chieachtaim aisream, séipéal, mosc.
Tearmann aimsím
sa pháirc fíogadán
ar Rinn Troisc i mBéara.

Ansin ar shlat mo dhroma dhom
is fearr a chloisim
macalla leighis:
Bíodh grá id chroí don uile ní.

Ar deireadh, an tsimplíocht sin Chríost
is fiúntaí, is deacra – grá crua.
Cad is fiú sainmhíniú?
Mair, a chailín, dreap.

The Camomile Field

In the end
what use
definition?

There is still Chernobyl,
the Middle East, 'peace process',
the whole warped world.

Take choice –
Buddha, Christ, Mahomet
or other ways not theirs,
something worthy here, there but . . .

Tower of Babel: apt symbol –
unbridled confusion, vision become
rampart never scaled.

Destruction, ruin, hate:
If I am mother I am guilty.
In flight am I
from the confusion within.

To no ashram, church, mosque
I go. Sanctuary I find
in the camomile field
in Rinn Trisk on Beara.

There, stretched flat on my back,
I best hear
a healing echo:
Let there be love in your heart for all.

In the end, this simplicity of Christ
is worthiest, most difficult – hard love.
What is the point of definition?
Live, woman, climb.

Revision

With hindsight, fifty years or so on,
one could conceive revised text for
marriage service. One would keep it light,
nothing like *to have and to hold until death*
for by then one would know having is relative
and holding there is none and until death
is negligible in a cracking world.

So much the better for one could realistically
put it this way: 'I plight my troth to the selves
we are of which we little know but cravings'.
Nothing so bleak, disloyal as *forsaking all others*.
The partner's reply: 'Wisely said. We shall aim
to chart some decency in the riot of choice.
Let us not possess each other'.

On the zenith of seventy plus one could be
thus distanced, thus inclined to rephrase
the wedding text. Incapacity or tolerance?
Too lived now, perhaps, for flaming pulse,
prospecting energy? And so, to pledge
nothing dreary, allowed latitude, yet
decent aim – such revision comes easy.

Eva Bourke

On Forgetting

Nous ne savons rien de la mémoire, rien, rien.
Sans oubli on n'est que perroquet. – Paul Valéry

Jamais n'oublierai cette fumée. – Elie Wiesel

Forget it. – Colloquial expression

I

It's nothing earthshaking in the beginning,
small lapses, you mislay things, keys, wallets,
forget numbers you ring everyday,
increasingly you can't place faces, recall names,
then you begin to take notice:
something is changing, something
is advancing towards you, no bigger yet
than the pin-point of a black star
just over the horizon, still far, still at a safe distance,
hardly making progress but marring the scenery,
the formerly untroubled perspectives.

You ask yourself, is this it, the beginning of the end
approaching almost imperceptibly
like a slight atmospheric disturbance,
the thin edge of the blade? You spot warning signals,
read about memory loss, Korsakov's syndrome, Alzheimer's,
you discover little that is new and that's mostly
speculation – the journals admit as much –
in your case it's simply a cluster of cells
in your frontal lobe system
slowing down their transmissions, a natural process
at your age. Wear and tear. That's no consolation.

You decide you're going to beat that thing,
not to give in lying down,
set yourself tasks, crosswords, memory drills,
learn historical chess games by heart,
(between Napoleon and one of his generals for instance
checkmated after losing his rook in the 36th move);
you memorise phone numbers, your children's, your doctor's
but forget your friend's husband's name; addresses,
birthdays you have to look up. Will the day come
when you can't remember the word 'apple'? There you are –
past 40, comical, sad, almost tragic, losing your grip on things.

You delve into the past, develop a mania
for keepsakes, memories, like a bloodhound
you track them down – father at the piano,
dead fish floating in darkgreen water,
GIs smile from the backs of army trucks,
chicken pox, cold wraps, eucalyptus and the scent
of mother's favourite soap –
half-remembered things that you take
by the scruff of the neck and force into the merciless light
of the present. Many things change fast,
you observe politicians and policemen get younger,

increasingly there seems to be less time, fewer emotions,
less love, fun, hope; you're baffled
by the latest technology, you stay in more,
watch chat shows on TV and lie awake at night wondering
what happened and what end your life is rushing towards.
You see your family more often: funerals
are becoming more frequent, death strikes closer to you.
You discover how irreplaceable the dead are, .
how huge the gaps they leave behind them.
You read books on forgetting. It remains a mystery.

Is is the mind simply dumping excess baggage to regain speed
or is it a sort of mental economics,
a jettisoning of odds and ends that weigh it down?
Why then can't it throw off things that once pained it
and are paining still? Why do certain moments
stay fixed in your memory, clear-edged and cutting as ever?
Still drawing blood? You are caught in a dilemma:
unable to forget what you most want to forget,
yet constantly trying to pin down what eludes you.
You feel like a badly tied travel bag
shedding its contents on a bumpy bus ride.

Distraught you take to drinking too much,
desiring what you fear in equal measures,
sometimes you think you've been struggling
up a mountain from which you look down on an ocean
that stretches past the horizon. On the strand
lies the boat you're going to paddle out onto the water.
So after your lifelong battle with keys and phone numbers,
appointments and punchlines,
this is the glistening void you will vanish into.
However, you can think of that with composure:
The sea and the boat are familiar metaphysical trappings.

But in one of your nightmares a flame runs along a fuse
through the grass towards you, speeding up
as it comes closer. You wake up sweat-drenched and shaking.
In the dream that follows, two of your dead loves
sit in a garden beside a sunlit river waving to you,
calling in birdlike indistinct voices.
You try to but can't hear what they're saying.
For a while you wonder what it was. Then you forget.
The grand finale is rarely dramatic, rather a little banal:
your hold on things sliding, colours getting dimmer, in the end
only the sound of a fuse crackling in the grass.

II

I, Charles Labussière, nicknamed the Chewer of Paris
actor and secretarial assistant
to the Committee for Public Safety
during the 'terreur'
saved approximately 1500 people from the guillotine
(among them Josephine de Beauharnais,
Napoleon's future wife as well as many actor friends)
by destroying their files.

Afraid of being caught – spies lurked everywhere –
I tore up the documents
printed on the official paper
of the Revolutionary Tribunal and ate them.
When my innards rebelled
(pulped rags and wood, gum, animal glue, ink)
I soaked the pages in a basin of water
kneaded them into papier machè balls
I could carry out in my pockets.
Disguised as an angler fishing for his breakfast
I dumped basketfuls of death sentences
into the Seine at dawn.
After the 'terreur' I returned to the stage.
First I was famous, a hero,
"le macheur de Paris" people flocked to see,
then I ceased to be news, my career faltered.
An actor friend writes a play about me.
Benefit performances
keep the wolf from the door for a while.
But the play being controversial
is taken off the programmes;
I took to drinking absinthe and vanished
in the bars and fleahouses of Montmartre.

I read this story last April in Vienna,
city of bad memories par excellence
behind its stately facades.
Unseasonal snow fell on Heldenplatz
and a Siberian wind shook the flagpoles.
Below golden domes, stone angels,
white as whipped cream, flailed their arms
on palace gutters.
We crossed the Danube stopping briefly
to look into the cold stream,
we knew the usual telltale odds and ends
would lie buried in the mud of the river bed:
road signs, party badges, grenade shells
give-away symbols of a sad and ugly past.

We stood for a while thinking we could hear
the river telling her non-stop stories:
that was in the year of the big crash
and later when the war came and the embargo starting biting
after most of our Jewish neighbours
had vanished – God knows where –
all we ever saw were turnips
turnip coffee, turnip bread, turnip schnapps
ah the smell of the bad old days
typhoid epidemics and a shortage of penicillin
not enough sterile dressings or
painkillers never enough painkillers
that year my mother turned my coat inside out
for the second and last time
the winter was icy
and we couldn't get fuel not one shovel of coal
in the whole of Vienna
remember how that year suicides
were ferried every day across the river
to the Graveyard of the Nameless
in the 11th district . . .

What is this thing – forgetting?
Perhaps you hope that at this moment
someone is tearing up your file
slowly, methodically,
soaking the shreds in a waterbasin,
carrying them out in his pockets
to dump them into the river,
the magical flood?
Is it asking too much of the executioner
to check through his lists

and not find your name written there,
and, having done his day's work,
to go home to his wife and child?

Last April after I read first about Charles Labussière,
strategist of merciful forgetting
in the city that never forgot
a single one of its victims,
I lay awake and thought of all
the millions who had vanished
thronging the streets
squeezing past shutters and latches
to make the same urgent request –
to keep their memories alive.

Place, date, name, sentence
the flourish of a signature on pages
torn from files, a verdict
dissolving in water,
slowly drifting downstream.
The angels gesturing to the sky
above dripping gutters
never reach the river.
They're condemned to look on,
petrified by memories of the fall,
while the chewer of Paris,
Charles Labussière in angler's disguise,
an empty basket beside him on the banks of the Seine
hauls a fish for breakfast from the water.

Seán Hutton

Leigheas ar Chrá Croí
Leagan de dhán as Berber le Sidi Rabia Ait Sidi Amar

Beanna arda na sléibhte
idir mise is mo chairde ionúine.
Nach fada iomardúil an bóthar
dá mbeadh a gcabhair ag teastáil.
Réitigh an bealach dom, a Dhia,
go bhféadfaidh mé lán mo dhá shúl
a bhaint as na cairde dílse
a chuireann mo thuairisc go rialta:
mar sin a leigheasfear mo thinneas
gan úsáid cógais ná ortha.

A Cure for Heart-Ache
A version of a poem in Berber by Sidi Rabia Ait Sidi Amar

The peaks of the high mountains
lie between me and my dear friends.
Is not the road long and dangerous
if their help were required.
O God, make smooth the way before me
so that I may feast my eyes
upon those true friends
who regularly ask for news of me:
that way my sickness will be cured
without the use of medicines or spells.

Aoir
bunaithe ar dhán le Catullus

A Chamadáin, nach agatsa atá an anáil bhréan!
A ghaotaire, nach n-oireann duit go seoigh
gach a dúradh riamh faoi lucht bladhmaireachta is ráiméise.
Nach smaoineofá ar úsáid níos fearr a bhaint as do theanga:
tóineanna agus cosa lofa ghramaisc do mholta a lí, mar shampla.
Cén fáth go gcaitheann tú an méid sin ama le huisce faoi thalamh –
ag iarraidh ár gclú a mhilleadh –
nuair nár ghá duit ach do chlab mór a leathadh
chun muid a dhíothú le drochbholadh.

Satire
based on a poem of Catullus

Twister, how your breath stinks!
Windbag, how neatly all that was ever said
concerning boasters and idiots applies to you.
Wouldn't you consider making better use of your tongue:
by licking the arses and stinking feet of your sycophants, for instance.
Why do you waste so much time
conspiring to destroy our reputations,
when, if you just opened your big mouth wide,
your rotten breath would instantly destroy us.

John F Deane

The Dead and the Undead of St Michan's

They attended us, like martyrs, for centuries
as if their bones were stone and the skin
cured leather; they stood like sand-shapes
abandoned by the tides, their language courtesy

and silence. We were witnesses to patience,
withheld decay, time-keepers tremulous
to be loosed onto the air; we shook hands
with Strongbow, Patrick, Jesus, Thor

and left again, awed, and less afraid.
Then they came in from our impatient streets,
our cider-drinkers, our language-killers,
they heaped the bones into a pyre, the skulls

void with a centuries' old screaming till –
with a communal sigh – they yielded
to the flames. Farewell, our old familiars,
our seafarers, our progenitors, our clowns.

The Mouth of Moving Water

Crossing the sound between the islands
was one of the shortest seafaring journeys
but required craft and dedication, a pitch

in the handling of sea-words; trawlers lean,
old dandies, against quay walls, on the pier
a languorous disarray of lobster-pots

makes you watch your foothold on the world. Once
there was a lighthouse answering other lights,
telephone wires whistled Atlantic airs; now

deserted houses nest in the low valley,
there's a schoolhouse where the western gales
repeat old rhymes by rote in the old language;

the people left, grown more luxurious,
and who could blame them? or blame
the traveller, returned, who looks across the sound

towards silence, space, the monastic plot,
and there's that glorious step that you could take
out of the land-locked to the sloping deck.

Vixen

The word is snarl and needle-tooth, though,
when we were startled by the sudden rush
in the whitethorns she seemed young, that glow
of the fur, the delicacy of the brush,

she was belly-tangled in a wire snare.
I had thought Lord Fox and I had parted ways
but here his kind was forcing me to share
in the ordering that circumscribes our days;

I could have cried at the yielding hang of her head,
the vulnerable sex-organs, the eyes
deep with the discovery of pain; instead
that immaculate patience, the soft cries

told how the mankind-shaken commonplace hour
revealed an accusing beauty. When we let her go
back into her otherwhere, she bore the sour
consonants of survival, the mushed vowels of sorrow.

The Taking of the Lambs

The ewes were shifting in the darkness,
exhaling sorrow in wooden dunts
of incomprehension; lightning silently
skittered on the horizon, the milky way
was a vast meandering sheep-track;
the gate was barred again and the hard
hooves of the ewes slithered in the glaur,
their legs too thin tonight to sustain
the awful weight of their bodies;
the sheep-dogs stretched, contented, soon
to be swore at again, curmudgeoned and cringing
and the dung-stained truck loomed in the yard;
that night was the shadow of a maker God
laid down on a naked world, and even the stars
obediently stepped out their side-shuffle dance
of destruction, the thunder eventually rolling down.

Peter Fallon

The Cloud Factory

As we drive past the mines
Adam says to me:
They're working hard
in the cloud factory.

Gate

There's no track of a hedge,
no trace of a fence.
In the middle of a field
an iron gate and no evidence

of path or passage.
It clings to rusty hinges
on chiselled stone,
it hardly infringes

on the course of stock –
for cattle a pair
of scratching posts,
for the colt and chestnut mare

a nuzzling place where you pause
and again you contemplate
in the middle of open grazing
your fate

by a gate that stops nothing
and points nowhere . . .
Say for a moment
the field is your

life and you come
to a gate at the centre
of it. What then?
Then you pause. And open it. And enter.

An Easter Prayer

The first forsythia;
daffodils;
gorse or whins or furze
on hills,

in hedges.
Late winter aconite;
dandelions; primroses
challenging the light

of Easter morning.
The lesser celandine;
a yellow fertilizer
bag define

Spring in our steps.
I love my children
and my wife.
Rise all again and again.

Eavan Boland

My Country in Darkness

After the wolves and before the elms
the Bardic Order ended in Ireland.

Only a few remained to continue
a dead art in a dying land:

This is a man
on the road from Youghal to Cahirmoyle.
He has no comfort, no food and no future.
He has no fire to recite his friendless measures by.
His riddles and flatteries will have no reward.
His patrons sheath their swords in Flanders and Madrid.

Reader of poems, lover of poetry –
in case you thought this was a gentle art,
follow this man on a moonless night
to the wretched bed he will have to make:

The Gaelic world stretches out under a hawthorn tree
and burns in the rain. This is its home,
its last frail shelter. All of it –
Limerick, the Wild Geese and what went before –
falters into cadence before he sleeps:

He shuts his eyes. Darkness falls on it.

Rosemarie Rowley

Dónal Óg
from the Irish

Dónal Óg, don't set your words astray
But take me with you when you cross the water
You'll have a fairing[1] on every market day
And you will sleep with the Greek king's daughter

You promised me and it was a lie
You'd wait for me at the sheep's paling
I whistled and called three hundred times my cry
And all I heard was a small lamb wailing

If you go without me I have your description
You have fair tresses and two green eyes
Twelve yellow curls in your hair, a depiction
The colour of a cowslip or a garden rose

It was late last night a dog barked where you stood
And the the snipe squawked of your presence in the marsh
You were deep in solitude in the wood
May you be without a wife even if this sounds harsh

You promised me something which came easy
A fleet of golden ships with silver masts
Twelve townlands and the market busy
And a limestone court near the sea headfasts[2]

You promised me something quite impossible
That you would give me gloves made of fish-skin
That you would give me bird-skin shoes, incredible
And a suit of Irish material the costliest, silken

It was early in the morning I saw a young man
Upon a horse, taking the road
He didn't come near me nor exert a ban
On returning home I cried a load

Ochone, and it isn't that I'm famished
For the want of food or drink or sleep –
the reason I'm skinny and almost vanished
My love for a young man has cut me deep

---

1. gift from the fair
2. mooring ropes for ships

Donal Og, I'd be better for you
Than a haughty woman puffed with pride
I'd do your milking and churning for you
And however hard the blows, I'd be at your side

When I go to the Well of Loneliness
I sit and cry till my heart's a stone
All life is around me, save a true caress
From he with amber shadow on his high cheekbone

It was upon a Sunday I gave you my love
The very Sunday before Easter Day
I was reading the passion on my knees, it behove
My two eyes sending you love all the way

My mother told me not to speak to you
Today, tomorrow or on the Sabbath
It was bad timing to be warned against you
The stable door closed: what's left is the ha'p'orth

O mother, please let me have him, please
And give him all in the world I possess
Even go out and beg for alms on your knees
Please don't prevaricate and deny me access

Black as the sloe is my heart inside each day
Black as a lump of coal in a smithy's forge
Black as a footprint in a shining hallway
As a dark mood overcoming humour's urge

You took the East and you took the West from me
You took my future and my past, it is hell
You took the moon and you took the sun from me
And, I greatly fear, you have robbed me of God as well.

Adrian Rice

The Book of Life

He loved that moment when family members,
Long lost friends or cherished lovers,
Forgot themselves in their rush to embrace.
For him it was a foretaste of Heaven's grace.
He would hide his teary eyes by sleight-of-hand,
By channel changing and manly banter
Or by slipping to the scullery to make us supper.
He would reappear with china teacups in each hand
And create a fuss deciding which was which.
Settled, he would swear that *This Is Your Life* was kitsch.
Now everything has turned titanic since his death.
As I soak, foam-ruffled, in the tepid water,
Even the *BE SURE* deodorant bottle
Lies like a toppled king upon the shelf.

Gerard Donovan

Untended View

One day I glimpsed Troy through a hedge-gap
in the field behind my house.
I grabbed a thorn in surprise,
followed flaming arrows. After an hour
I left them to that business with the walls,
milked the cow into a tin bucket.
The din died down. I made tea.

This evening I peruse a book at Dingle Strand,
tales in small type, cold stout at my lips.
I've read to Herodotus, Xerxes' Persian march
(where an army took six days to pass).
I'm glad to be out of that boredom, the goings on.
A horse gallops, cuts the waves:
is it Godiva or my daughter?
Grass blows in and out of history.

One day the skies might crack open,
flood my fields with jumbled creeds and heroes.
But now I lie in open view of the past,
held prisoner by pocketfuls of air.
Find me, old laws, old orders.

Ernest Bates

A River in Spate

Fresh as a levelled grave
Flood waters of the Suir
Dun cow-hide stretched between trees.

January Fill-Dyke

A calling crane combs slowly from the south
A hunter searching for a submarine
In air-force camouflage of grey by grey
Quarters and requarters the escutcheon
Of foamless flood that fills the lap of the weir
Clever as a quill, draws thirty quarterings
Then for a flourish describes two more,
One for every county in Ireland.

Eugene O'Sullivan

Ballade of Indigenous Inquietude

I

Is this Pictish interpreter loyal?
    I don't see these hills on the map.
Should we call their chiefs Noble or Royal?
    Shall we stroke them, or give them a slap?
Are they classified P-Celt or Q-Celt?
    Are they dim, or uncommonly bright?
Are their coverings woad, or just blue felt?
    The natives are restless to-night.

II

So they say they've declared independence
    (In gibberish noisome and high).
They proclaim themselves English descendants.
    They'll sell anything money can buy.
They commit representative treason,
    And call it a God-given right,
Or insist they are driven by Reason.
    The natives are restless to-night.

III

My wife says she dreamed I must free him.
     He says he's a king, but not here.
The rules say that Herod should see him.
     Surely he, and not I, should show fear?
What is truth, for that truth seems to fill him?
     Pain is darkness, he looks living light.
Caesar's friend has no choice but to kill him –
     The natives are restless to-night.

Envoi

Prince, the prices you charge are outrageous!
     Your bed-conversation is trite.
Your diseases may well be contagious –
     The natives are restless to-night.

Jean O'Brien

The Carrier

I hold my daughter close,
loving the lines of her body.
She carries my fingerprints,
I carry her history.

In the angle of her head,
that I can cup with my two hands,
lies the future.
She will be the death of me.

I carried her below my heart
for nine short months,
she will carry me forever.

I am running along the lines
of her blood. I am tapped
into her bone. I am the echo
in her head.

Child C

I am the child that carries the child,
a Russian doll, a hawthorn hedge.

The flower and the thorn. We are hemmed in
with white flowers. I am a named child

who bloomed early. A May blossom
is burgeoning inside me.

Above our heads they talk a language;
some mad boolean algebra

in trimesters and letters
that fetter me here.

I was bridging the chasm between
child and woman

when he tore through me, planting
his seed, battering my senses and flesh.

I like a firefly then, burning the bushes
scorching the white blossoms, stripping the bark

When the bough breaks
we all fall.

Fred Johnston

Progress

All the crass machines have gone to sleep
Morning is as quiet as an old battlefield

We wake up too young in the world
Full of nonsense about a new millennium

How long before they drag down the tree
Through which we've watched the winter moon?

False Coin

A small shop in a Bann village:
"That's the wrong money – there,
That's us now."

Plucking the Queen's coin from
A palmful of harps and horses,
Flicking salmon,

Used to all sorts here; a mill,
Stern in its rotting red brick,
A steeple on a hill.

Nailed-up doors spell out
A sentence of economic death,
With no hope of reprieve.

Yet the view from a high window
Is wonderful, novelesque:
Green trees, a river bridge.

Nothing tribal dogs the place,
Thank God for that. Neglect
Wears neither harp nor bowler hat.

Nancy Doyle

You are Not a Thing

We walk around you, demure as novices
with downcast lids, our feet
nimble and quick as antelope,
lest we should somehow be snared
into seeing you, hearing you croak
"Molly Malone" as you rock.

You are itinerant. I suspect
you are woman like me but, under the streel
of rust hair, it is hard to be sure.
If I stop to look, to hand you
my pocketful of silver, I would begin to worry
where you will sleep tonight.

I know you are not a thing. But I must pretend
so I can skirt you neatly, achieve
the far side of the Ha'penny Bridge, before
you can put out a dirty paw,
claim me as sister.

Wood Quay

I would not like to have lived then
      in Winetavern Street.
      Dirty cold it must have been there
      between the grey Liffey
      and grey Christ Church where a small
leather boot has been teased free, another
      childish thing tapping out ready grief,
      leaving us to wonder if he died
      of plague in one of those wattle huts
      when Dublin was a Danish town.
I would not like to have lived then but O,
      to come back when I've been eons dead
      and watch the archeologists excavating,
      finding perhaps my son's blue
      slipper, lost under the stairs.

Pearse Hutchinson

From the Italian of Sandro Penna (1906-77)

To a latrine cool in the railway station
I come down from the scorching hill.
My skin is drunk on dust and sweat.
The sun still sings in my eyes.
To the shining white porcelain
I abandon body and soul.

River
(for Sujata Bhatt)

She plucked a flower and leaving the village
walked as far as the river.
She stood for a minute, watching the water move,
then bending down she placed – not cast –
the flower on the water.
Standing there for a short while, relaxing,
she watched the river carry the flower away,
till it was out of sight beyond the trees.
Then she walked back home.

A Findrum Blackbird

Were there nightingales here before the adze-head
    croziered?
and maybe she left us
        along with the serpent?
How should a snake and a nightingale con*sort*?
She hardly wrenned it on his eagle-back,
unless he was Mexican – or did she guide him
back to the garden of eden?

But never mind, we have the blackbird still –
de Ierse nachtegaal, as Johann Jacob van Eyck
might well have called him,
peddling all over Flanders unearthly flute-music –
what nightingale could ever sing
so well as that blind wanderer?

Perched acrest a lilac-bush
just inside the front gate
black-and-yellow music
turns a garden into a glade-scriptorium,
brings back those pagan monks,
and fills my deaf harmonious kitchen-window
with yellow-and-black music.

Patrick Galvin

Poem for my Children

My two children
Play soldiers by the sea,
I tell them
To look to the horizon
And listen carefully
To the mouths of gulls.

My children listen
But all they can hear
Is the grieving sound of gunfire.

My daughter, Grainne,
Breathes nightmares of gunfire
And my son, Macdara, is convinced
That the Earth is made of shrapnel
And bone.

I tell them
The sun is a lamp
To be held lightly
In the palm of the hand.

Sometimes,
My children sing
A Revolutionary Song –
They say they heard it in a dream
And they ask how long it will be
Before the last glimmering sun
Explodes over dry waters.

I tell them
The world is a magic carpet
I tell them
To rise and dance in the rain
I tell them
To listen to the gulls

And
Sleep peacefully
In their Mother's
Arms.

Rachel

The blossoms in her arms were white
She carried the atonement of her race
And there was no sound
No protest
As they stumbled awkwardly
Towards the flame.

The legions of the night wore black
The lake is a furnace of rain.
Why do you lean on the dark, Rachel?
Why do they call you my name?

The trees in the orchards are burning
The leaves are the greening of bone.
Why are you crossed with a star, Rachel?
Why do you bleed here alone?

They have sprinkled your head with ashes
Your shawl is a prayer for the dead.
Why are you wearing my heart, Rachel?
Why do you weep at my bed?

The blossoms in her arms are red
She carries the atonement of her race
And there is no sound
No protest
As we stumble awkwardly
Towards the flame.

Lost John

Under this stone lies Lost John
He was strange as anyone.

I am Lost John
I have no face
I belong to no race
Lost John
Of no place.

I was born of loss and dree
No breast to tender me.
Those who made me were shorn
Those who named me soon gone.
I am Lost John.

I make faces of blue stone
Looking-glass of skin and bone

But I never can see
Where Lost John should be –
Tell me.

I walk with knobbled stick
No roof or bed of tick
No mark of where I've been
No lake to wash me in –
I am Lost John.

I look on God's face
I ask of him a place.
What I see in men's eyes
Is naught but lies.
Suffer me.

I sleep in harrowed ground
No bones of me be found.
She who buried me not known
He who fathered me has flown.
I am Lost John.

Michael Hartnett

for the Hartnetts
Based on the German of Heinrich Heine

We felt very deeply for each other
and, strange to tell,
we got on very well.

We often played at 'Husband and Wife'
and, strange to tell,
we did not bicker, we did not fight;
our jokes we happily shared,
we kissed, we embraced.

And, in the end, with young delight,
we played 'Hide and Seek' in wood and lane.

We became so good at going ahide
that we never found each other again.

For Máire Newton

Slowly the blossoms are falling
on the Huguenots;
and earlier on, for every soul,
a bluebell wet and waxy
springs up to tax the Dublin sky
that lacks, most summers,
the perfect azure that they longed for.
Slowly the blossoms are falling
on the armour of their version
of their God
as they lie in Merrion Row,
and pile up like shrouds of snow;
and three miles north of them
the Jewish bodies rest
and dream of possible heavens
(but, at least, no hell, at best);
and sleep soundly with their wish
to know they do not know.
Let us
always stop and pray
for people who meant well;
who rest in their several ghettos,
who believed or disbelieved in Hell;
who hear and do not heed

a voice of bronze and iron tell
at eight and twelve and six o'clock
the numbers of the Irish dead
who heard their version of their God
in the Angelus bell.
Yaweh, Allah, Father
ye're up to yere old tricks.
Slowly the blossoms fall
on the Catholics.

A Prayer for Sleep

Grant me good rest to-night, O Lord;
let no creatures prowl
the tangled pathways in my skull;
wipe out all wars,
throw guilt a bone;
let me dream, if I dream at all,
no child of Yours has come to harm.

I know, of course, that death's the norm;
that there are people who have yet to climb
the Present's rungs, who lag behind
(hyaenas at the rim of civilization's light)
whose laughing hides a Stone Age howl,
who wait till darkness comes to pounce
and tear the guts of progress out.

Yet, grant me good rest to-night, my Lord,
blind my internal eyes;
guard my anxious baffled years
with Your protecting arm
and let me dream, if I dream at all,
no child of Yours has come to harm.

Seamus Heaney

The Little Canticles of Asturias

1

And then at midnight as we started to descend
Into the burning valley of Gijon,
Into its blacks and crimsons, *in medias res*,
It was as if my own face burned again
In face of the fanned-up lip and crimson maw
Of a pile of newspapers lit long ago
One windy evening, breaking off and away
In flame-posies, small airborne fire-ships
Endangering the house-thatch and the stacks –
For we almost panicked there in the epic blaze
Of those furnaces and hot refineries
Where the night-shift worked on in their element
And we lost all hope of reading the map right
And gathered speed and cursed the hellish roads.

2

Next morning on the way to Piedras Blancas
I felt like a soul being prayed for,
Giddy and replenished all at once.
I saw men cutting aftergrass with scythes,
Beehives in clover, a windlass and a shrine,
The maize like golden cargo in its hampers.
I was a pilgrim new upon the scene
Yet entering it as if it were home ground,
The Gaeltacht, say, in the nineteen fifties,
Where I was welcome, but of small concern
To families at work in the roadside fields
Who'd watch and wave at me from their other world
As was the custom still near Piedras Blancas.

3

San Juan de la Cruz
Had his dark night of the soul.
At San Juan de las Harenas
It was bright day.
Two rivers flowed together under sunlight.
Watercourses scored the level sand.
The sea hushed and glittered outside the bar.
And in the afternoon, the cockleshells
I threw together in a casual pile
Bobbed and flashed on air like altar boys
With their quick turns and tapers and responses
In the great re-echoing cathedral gloom
Of distant Compostela, *stela, stela*.

Francis Devine

A Red Flag Rhyme

for Jim Connell and Tommy Grimes

Back to the land they came,
from Fulham Broadway and Finglas West,
Wandsworth, Waterford and Willowfield,
through the springing, rainbowed meadows of Meath,
where he once trapped, tickled and reclaimed
beyond the bailiffs' scrutiny and lordly injustice:
they came to celebrate the man,
the big man in the Inverness Cape,
him with the cascading moustaches and hot whiskey eyes,
he who wrote *The Red Flag* and wept
when Ramsay MacDonald managed to ruin his poem.

Marching beneath the bloody shades of his talent,
they lit up the countryside from Kells to Kilskyre,
Frenchmen and sturdy Germans, Inuit and Koori people,
Hottentot and Hispanic, Orange and Green,
a mighty wave that rolled back history's rotten pages
to reveal that the writing of the times was yet to be done,
would value those that walked anonymously
in among the throng – Hardie and Hannington,
Macgougan and Mann, Connolly, Quelch and Scott –
would ask of them strategic initiatives that would cement
his thoughts from Charing Cross to New Cross
in some more glorious verse of succeeding action
that would allow us all – come Millennium –
to truly raise his scarlet standard high,
high enough to scrape and spark the very stars.

Michael Longley

The Iron Bird

Helen Denerley made this raven out of old iron,
Belly and back the brake shoes from a lorry, nuts
And bolts for legs and feet, the wings ploughshares
("Ridgers", she elaborates, "for tatties and neeps"),
The eyeballs cogs from a Morris Minor gearbox.

The bird poses on the circular brass tray my mother
(and now I) polished, swipes of creamy Brasso,
Then those actions, melting a frosty window pane,
Clearing leaves from a neglected well, her breath
Meeting her reflection in the ultimate burnish.

The beak I identified first as a harrow tooth
Is the finger from an old-fashioned finger bar
Mower for dividing and cutting down the grass,
And, as he bends his head to drink, the raven points
To where the surface gives back my mother's features.

Peter Sirr

The Instruction

Don't sing about your city, leave it in peace
Song is not the movement of machines or the secret of houses.
– Carlos Drummond de Andrade

Released from the mind
like bread on water:
pigeons, cats,
the torment of kitchens,

the inner lives of chefs;
left to their own devices
the man in his window,
the exhaust from buses.

I walk in the absent park
by the vanished lake.
At last, nothing: the
long sleep of stone;

the sky on its knees, praying
for the repose of monuments,
the ease of churches, fishmongers;
avenues of emptiness,

the pavements sunk;
nights plagued
by ghosts of swans,
the adulteries of motorists,

the confessions of streetlamps,
the insistent
intricate and tender
movement of machines . . .

Cathedral

I dyd byllyd and pyllyd with oke timber
I fyllyd hit the foundacion with roche lyme.
The masons paid, the carters paid
the smith, the cooper, the casters of sand.

What I really wanted was to stand
for once empty handed
by the vanishing spires and the bells
beautifully dumb, pealing quiet

as we waited, the world rinsed out of us.
Stone by stone the city returned
these streets mapped by desire
the light that seemed to flare

from our own skin to press
the district towards us.
As if in a small rain of touch
we stood, and watched it grow.

I leaned towards you, provoking
a dark bricked brewery palazzo
you kissed me and caused
black tramlines to loop and veer.

When you stopped, they disappeared.
So greedy the desire
the whole place seemed to fall
and my spirit, that had been light, was air.

Home

Nearby, the crumbling palace;
nearby, the famous station
held up by fierce angels;

chewing-gum clings
to the bus-park tarmac
like an old faith;

the ice-breaker Strength
waits for winter
at the end of the street;

someone puts his face in the sky
to suck a herring,
someone finds his wallet's gone;

at night the graveyards loosen,
the dead walk their streets again,
their mouths filled with names,

stones falling from their eyes;
and the routes oblige:
apartment buildings, hotels

crumble in their palms; a sigh
of concrete, sudden bones of steel,
the cleared ways tangled again,

coiling round repeatedly and always
an alley, a fencepost, a huckster's entrance
short of recognition; all night

the city multiplies; all night
sails out from itself and, bloated, returns,
each street its own harbour;

the dead walk their water;
from a quay wall I lean,
eyes sweeping the scene, as if

through glass, through water, through stone
something unshakeable might shine
and fix: the city disrobed, inviting;

milk gleam of the known
street, the familiar house;
in the depths, in the deepest dark

of the innermost room a stillness
living and dead have drifted towards;
silent transaction, bones lent,

reconfigured, limbs tested, stretched,
sleep bartered with sleep,
the light, when it comes, changing hands.

Conor O'Callaghan

Reprise

Yet again September yields
the year's only scorcher,
and we are peeling apples
from a dying man's orchard.

The Bypass

There are no ships in the
        docks. It has been raining.
It falls to us like this with each successive week,
the vague sense of being cut adrift or drowning
that sleeplessness accentuates.
        Then a while back
it dawned on me that we
        had made our home on land
that is reclaimed. Ever since I have been at sea.
They have cut a bypass over the Lower End,
from the halting sites to
        the bird sanctuary.
It is the latest in
        a long stream of removes
from the outside world. It is finished. It crosses
Seatown within earshot of here in even waves
between the tool hire yard
        and the early houses.
It has given our lives
        an edge. It's out there now,
going through the motions of distance and darkness,
matter-of-fact, an orchard ripening yellow,
making time and deadlines
        and midsummer starless,
a latter-day silk route
        murmuring with fireflies,
piling itself up at traffic lights, pointillist,
then shifting through its gears, beautiful and tireless,
a droning scarcely
        audible though always just,
like moths at the window
        or next door's radio
left running for months, a heavy relentless hum
that quickens past eight and we turn in and wake to,

not once diminishing
                      or losing momentum,
whether hauliers in
                      articulated trucks
or joyriders at speed or motorbikes in swarms
or sirens ebbing on the old shore like tidemarks
or Saturday's tail-back
                      exhaling its sweet fumes,
a necklace lying away
                      out on the marshes
and the mile of disused industrial estates,
linking cities, migrant, a river that washes
its own hands of silence,
                      that dusk accelerates,
that almost dries to a
                      standstill if never quite,
day and night and day and night, not once letting up,
half-dreamt, a buzz constantly in my head of late
and even yet as I
                      write it will never stop.

Baltray

What day survives has yet to give, and may never.
The golf links ruffles a solitary number four.

The dunes are out of bounds, the grey lines gaining,
the lamp standards at the mouth of the estuary.

This is all by the way, all ancient history.
The word translates itself farther still from meaning

until the names for home and here are nothing more
than different tributaries of the same river.

Rody Gorman

Malairt

Chan eil mi ach a' tabhann
Mo ghaoil dhut mar bhathar;
Cha leig thu leas a cheannach ann,
Cha leig, chan eil e gu diofar:
Tha na riaghailtean-malairt àbhaisteach
A' bualadh air a' ghnotach.

Commerce

I am merely offering
My love for you as a commodity;
There is no obligation to purchase,
No obligation whatsoever:
The usual rules
Of commerce apply.

Sùibheagan

Chaidh mi air ais an-uiridh
Dhan achadh os cionn a' chladaich

Dhan d'rachadh mo chuideachd a thogail shùibheagan
Ach 's e fhuair mi romham ach smeuran,

Astar beag air falbh bhon chladh
San deach an tiodhlacadh.

Strawberries

I went back last year
To the field above the shore

Where my folks used to go picking strawberries
But all I found was brambles,

A wee bit from the graveyard
Where they're buried.

Colette Connor

Poor Lily

*"Far away places, with strange-sounding
names, far away over the sea . . ."*

Remember the song, Lily?
You used to sing it when you were young
and dream how one day you would go over
the sea and find out for yourself.

"Poor Lily, left on the shelf",
your family said. "Never found a man
to take her to his bed. It all went
wrong inside her head. Poor dead Lily!"

Poor Lily. How strange and far away
your family were. How peculiar.

Foxtrots and Tangos

That year you left Manchester for London,
found a room to rent in Hammersmith,
went to work on the building sites
erecting houses, row on row of brick.
In between you lived your other life:
each night you changed into a gigolo,
to partner single women and widows
in waltzs, foxtrots and tangos,
shimmy shimmering across the hall,
starlit in the Palais Ballroom.
You must have looked a rare specimen,
neat feet slipped in patent leather shoes,
black hair gleaming, eyes of china blue,
your heart of darkness hidden
beneath a devil-may-care attitude.
Who knows how many women
you romanced during that brief interlude
as you danced to the distant beat
of home and the woman who waited –
the one you had yet to meet.

Kevin Kiely

Elegy for a father
(d 1963)

Mother in black clothes, left us with Mrs Kelly
A crowd came from the burial after mass
That year JFK's visit was the big news on telly
And then the shots at Dallas
In our eyes glints of grief were seen
They made condolences to the widow
And four children aged six to thirteen
The Examiner's front page photo
Showed the burnt out gate lodge of Drishane Convent
We bought extra copies for relatives
Your death notice was inside
What had I said
About the dead?
To you in your sickbed
Sitting on an upright chair
Coat, scarf and cap over your pyjamas
How you held us close, each in turn
Precious father, Chestertonian man
Dick Barrett and Dermie Murphy
Lifted you down the house steps
To the Ford consul taxi for Mallow hospital
You never came home and you never died
Clara mountain is on view
From the sloping cemetery at Millstreet
The Fionnabha is full of fish in season
While your shade is always here
Perhaps I'll go on with you
Arriving home finally
To the unknowable destiny
of the Deity

Art Murphy

Balm

1

After the war Rene Maguire painted nudes
as fleshy and amorphous as clouds.
He treated canvases as 2-dimensional
for the theme of his art was the curve
and he explored it through all its orbits
with the compassion of the Lord Buddha.

2

Marguerite Keenan, my mother's cousin,
washed the dead of John Mitchel Street
on their kitchen tables. She sponged them
with warm soapy water and bawdy humour –
laid them out in shrouds as flawless
as the harvest moon above the graveyard wall.

3

The Madden brothers dressed local granite
and imported white marble for headstones.
Their incised gold lettering was under-
written by wind's recursive signatures
and when they'd buffed the stone until it shone
rain found as little purchase there as fingers.

Vona Groarke

The Dream House

Downstairs is all civility and grace.
The rooms proceed with well-intentioned flow
that takes in practicality and show.
Everything is in its ordained place.

The clock predicts familiar time.
The chairs are settled where they always were.
The chimney is untroubled by a fire,
and nothing stirs for any move of mine.

I am following my guide, as I must do,
in silence, while he talks me through the plan.
I am ushered in, informed and then moved on,
through lower rooms in a house I do not know.

We round back on the hall. I know it now –
the difficult stairs, the family oils
arranged in three-four time along the walls,
the faces that refuse my wary eye.

As we ascend, something seems to change.
The mood of certainty falters. There's a mirror
in which I am caught, for a moment, somewhere
between surprise and reassurance. I look strange.

He gives me fewer facts: he grows more quiet.
I begin to see for myself. The doors are ajar.
I choose the nearest and notice that the curtains are
the colour of my eyes. In certain light.

He opens the wardrobe. I see clothes that I might wear:
shoes in my size in a row under the bed.
On the shelf, some books I'd like to read,
and when I look behind me, a closed door.

The house is all beyond me, the room recedes.
I begin to lose the sense of what I saw.
In all this detail, one apparent flaw:
my unlost earring crumpled on the sheets.

Eibhlín Evans

Abroad

(For Anne, Eavan, Eiléan, Leland, Mary, Medbh, Nuala, Paula et al)

You sit here waiting for me
and my heart quickens at the sight
of you lying close together,
your slim spines showing
through the covers. Elegant and slight,
belie the expansive
pleasure of your speaking out. Out.

For you know the space between *babóg*[1]
and Baubo is a lifetime's pain.
Realise the moment
when the first lascivious crone
cheered Demeter,
made her laugh,
and brought her daughter home.

I'm glad to be with you
nestling into your lines
and cupping all your contours
like some bewildered child,
dreaming the prize,
going with you to Thesmophoria[2]
part of the rooftop rite.

To find myself,
laid out
my naked pulses sung
and come among you
for like you,
I like to hold
my own bold tongue.

---

1. *babóg:* Irish: doll. Baubo: Early Greek mythological figure who is said
to have cheered the grieving Demeter through acts of a lascivious nature
and the telling of raucous stories.
2. Early Greek women-only festival of fertility rites.

Hugh Maxton

Agamemnon Road, NW6
(for Jane Haville)

Close by Fortune Green
The muse is no longer news.
Hell is to be seen

Hades at the least
Sign of remission
From life's disease –

Texaco burning through
The loose-leaf trees,
The nondescriptive blue.

Besieged, I build a bookshelf
In our tilting house
And browse for my self in

Theology's exacting
Fictions of here and now
Truly unpacked.

Quicks and sparrows
Of the hedge school
(Either-way dead authors)

Their titles loll in rows
Each a dusty answer
Lies or epic, just prose.

The poetry best follows
If as much may do
Duty by bright shadows –

Ink of Pope's translation,
The Dean's heroic fear,
Mal-flowering spleen.

A Trojan on parole, I espouse
No widowed future here.
Exile's too good for me, allows

Love with love's painful sighs
On the inaudible air.
We walk beneath uncommon skies.

A Bad Joke
('Non senex, sed Sanex.')

Bubbles like bloodvessels
Brighten the surface.

Two frowning sunflowers
Stand back-to-back for hours.

The space between us
Burns with light, with light and loss.

Brendan Kennelly

Raindrop

Did I ever think I'd come to this?
Alone on a third-storey window
with the wind extorting

homage from the trees, bowing
in submission to the patient
graces of the evening,

not a bird in sight
and a grumpy, dangerous slant
to the summer light.

Yes, I said summer. Maybe that's why
I'm alone up here
above the belligerent city,

transparent as the glass I squat on.
Any moment now, I could be
running down the visible world

to meet my destiny,
kiss it and say
"My dear, you look *so* dry."

What will my destiny say?
Has it cheek enough to tell
a solitary raindrop to go away,

merge with the universe,
get lost? I think not. Destinies can be
surprisingly shy,

almost afraid at times,
trembling at the prospect of contact.
Once I get moving, I love to act

my part in the cosmic play.
I frolic with the sun,
become a jewel in the eyes of men,

get tossed like a childbird in a storm
yet manage to land
somewhere, cool, fluid, strangely firm.

That's how I am just now
so why should I complain
of sudden, cold or heavy rain,

this friend of mine,
colleague, brother, sister,
means of transport, end and origin

on a third-storey window high above
rich prose of violence,
rhymed mysteries of love?

freckle

I live under
the deep light of her eye.
A few have looked at me with wonder

but most gloss over me in the light of day.
Her skin is my privilege.
I'm a tiny hedgebird near a highway's

insanely ordered traffic.
I reflect her in the whole of her health.
I measure her when she's sick.

I thrive at the edge of her daring.
I share the names in her dreams.
I ripple and skip in her singing.

I see her dispensing her light.
I'll witness her ageing,
be with her when she's not

here anymore.
That's how I see it anyway.
Maybe I'm wrong.

Maybe I'll wither like a bit of skin,
drift off into a freckleheaven
purged of my original sin,

transfigured into that state of grace
I spend each moment of my tiny life
loving in her face.

Gabriel Fitzmaurice

On First Looking into Brendan Kennelly's Poetry My Arse

There is a poem that can't be told in church,
A poem that sings its truth just as it is,
A poem that pulls the preacher from his perch
As he holds on for dear life to certainties;
A poem that confesses to its sin
But out in public – not in some black box;
A love-cry from the depths to let grace in,
So full of life, an outrage!, that it shocks.
Tone it down!, the pious cry in mock
Indignation, knowing that full well,
This show of goodness, this pretence at shock's
The hypocrisy that Christ condemned to hell.
The poem shakes the church from off its feet
And leaves to sing itself out in the street.

Chris Agee

Thistledown

A gnomon falls a shade past XII on the Hospital's
Sun-dial at Kilmainham. How far am I now? Maybe
Nel mezzo del cammin – this noon at least,

Still fit at forty-two? Above it Anglican gold
Numbering our own clock's linear round. And higher still
The steeple-vane's golden Cockerel and Four Directions

Capped by the sailing white leviathans of a bright day
Whose sweeping windrushes shadow
In and out over the hot plaque of the Courtyard's suntrapped

Dust and gravel like pages turned now and then
In a book of light – or a white road at night gleaming
Polarized in an old vineyard of *la France profonde*. Past

The aluminium flagpole whose stick shadow right-angles
The jib of an invisible dhow: past the de Chirico arcade
Whose shadowland cuts light out of shade: Jacob gallops again

Towards the Great Hall's façade – strafed by Crimean redcoats –
In some endless enchanted Alamo of the spendthrift
Imagination. Strange how I never noticed the numerals

Descend on the right from VI to I
But ascend on the left from XII to VII
As if the ornate curlicues of the gnomon's idea

Topping my son were the parallel lives of light and dark
Unfolding and folding. For a moment the moment
Revives a crystalline June evening at the Giant's Ring

Where he ran wild on Indian paths through silage
Thick with buttercups and the purplish tinge of timothy-ears;
Then, upstairs in the old wards where he might have caught an eye,

The five green pears around a white plate in Scott's
Stilled zen-lifes of colour and form. As he runs on into new memory
Between the West Gate and the East, scuffing up dustiness,

Ghostly glints of the field-lint of thistledown
Sail around him like a tumbleweed of souls fleeing from
The child massacre at Omagh already happening three hours later.

Mark Roper

Face

When boiling soup splashed up
to scald your cheek, that was
one shock. When people moved
to avoid your bandaged glare
in a bar, that was another.
Face changed, you were changed.

As a child I wondered which face
I'd wear in heaven: my then face,
my adult one, my old age one?
And what about parents, friends?
Which ones would they be wearing?
How would anyone be known?

Faces won't matter, I was told,
spirits don't have them.
Even then I suspected no one
could exist without flesh:
face, spirit were not separate
nor would either be saved.

On the tiny field of new skin
around your eye, a soft gold down
grows again. When you're cold
or tired, the slight scar darkens:
as if this face had been signed
by its maker, its own death.

Robert Greacen

Thunderstorms

As if I'd pointed Uncle George's gun
The sheepdog cowered under the table.
God's moving his furniture, they said.
The Ulster air charged with electrons
Flashed and flushed to strike me dead
For I had stolen a biscuit from a tin.
The rumbles spoke of Calvinistic doom.

Years after, at something like sixteen
I stood erect beside my Uncle Jack
On his shaved English lawn.
I watched him laugh at flash and fury
As the rain dowsed clean our heads –
Freemason man and questing youth –
Until a rainbow blessed us both.

Ciaran O'Driscoll

Snow

Snow comes against me,
drifts past me,
touches me, a flake
lodges on the lid
of my lazy eye,
another on the lid
of my good eye, blinding me
with perfect crystals.
I wipe them away
and snow comes against me,
touches me without
the interest of an animal,
particles of a world
that might have been
falling dispassionately
on the world that is.
Everywhere I look
drifts of gravely
swaying memories,
shreds of innocence
gliding past me.

I walk a brown earth path
bordered by brambles,
acres of faded grass
and winter's besom trees
on one side, on the other
suburban gardens brought
to burglar-proof ends,
the former gateways sealed
by rusting sheets of metal,
and snow on every side
shaken endlessly out
of a nowhere cavern,
gliding through this gallery
of the artwork of the damned,
their signatures grown monstrous
to become the entire content,
Queenie, Pigeon, Lisa,
Woody, Jacko, Tommy,
names that fall like sleet
in public memory,
and snow comes against me,
touches me without
the interest of an animal.

Justice has not been done
and yet the heavens fall,
the flesh of Cassiope,
her fragments from the sky,
and all the flesh divided
and blown among the stars
comes floating back to earth
as neither flesh nor star,
totally other, strange,
sealing with perfect crystals
the good and the lazy eye,
falling dispassionately,
and snow comes against me,
drifts past me,
doesn't heed me,
doesn't need me,
if I stay will cover me.

Macdara Woods

Robert

Don't bully me
Hedli
I'll not be bullied
said Robert MacBryde
as we all of us lay
in a summer field
beneath Timoleague
in the 'sixties
watching tiny tractors climb
up and down the hill
across the valley

Don't bully me Hedli
I'll not be bullied –
that and:
Observation is my business

Death beat him
down
in Leeson Street
a few years after
bullied him into the ground
with all his
changeling gifts
of language and laughter
and dancing close
to what we mean by love:

And there's no way
round it
no going back
no way there
sweet man or not –

Just to jump and catch
to catch and hold
the image
for a moment
high above the street –

And see just now where
a hearse goes by

        a hearse with coffin
and no cortege

Mindscapes
(for my mother)

You dreamt
you were left in a field
all night
in a shed in a field
a bothán
on the Old McConnells'
land:
    the ones who hid
the half-moon parings
of their nails
and their folded locks
of hair
in hollow places
in the walls:
    but which of us
wouldn't
prefer to lie out
in a field at night
to be gone from here
and wake with leaves
about the bed
    recalling mysteries
the old road
underneath a ditch
the line
between the farms
a rough-flagged path
where mushrooms grew
from stones: as I
    remember it
you warn me now
of nettles
stinging plants

    and the cure
grows near the cause –

I think of this
and walk
into the sea today
along an
eighteenth century road –
the lines
beneath the earth

the rowan tree
the human heart

the cure
beside the cause

Patrick Deeley

The Workbench

Countless hammer-blows struck,
axe chippings, scrape-marks
of saw, vice-grip indentations,
plane and chisel scars, burrowings
made by bit and nail.

How many of these dealings
were intentional? Few, I'd say.
Should we put them down to slippage,
then, miscalculation, failure of the eye
to find its vision?

When you set to work, each
hand-made implement falling
fractions short of machine-won
finesse, I recognise the beauty
of little blemishes:

the finished article comes fresh
and distinct, drawing
an antique's endearments. And indeed
there are welts, reboundings
off the tasks.

But the workbench is stout enough
to take them all, to absorb
and wear the hardship, so further
particularising itself, through each
new thing you shape.

King of the Wood

Winter egg-breakfasts. We saved
the shells to helmet twigs of Spring.
Which was a whitethorn tree,
buttered and creamed with primroses

from the ditches, and danced around.
Our childhood, if we but knew,

a wilding dolled up in pagan ritual,
a throaty echo of the barbarian's

lost hurrah. He threw shapes
with us there, our woodman father,
stubble on his chin and sawdust

in his hair. His old credulousness

from before the calendared moon,
the unreliable sun configured
to clock, had been gradually tempered
to a gentle wisdom. He became

tranquil as the wood, his speech
so many silver-grey ash trunks
stealing upward to leaf-canopies
of interlinking boughs. In his face,

the sun's luminosity was occluded
now, now a sparring opulence.
Once, he lifted a hand to shade
my eyes, and it grew green-blooded.

Paddy Bushe

Oyster-Catchers on Uist

for Séamus Ó Catháin

"In Uist the oyster-catcher is called 'Bridein', bird of Bride"
— Carmina Gadelica

When I had read that, I could see
the long miles of sand, and the birds
in a black and white fuss of scurrying
and dibbling between the *machair* flowers.

Then, maybe I disturbed them, but
suddenly, as if a bell had sounded,
there was a great flurry of wings
and they were off, wheeling and cheeping

and cheeping and wheeling until it all
gathered into one limpid consonance.
I could imagine a settlement of sisterhood,
delighted into dancing, in circles widening

and widening forever, and forever singing
Bríd, Bríd, under a great blue cloak of sky.

Bolus

I. M. Máire Uí Chinnseala

At Bolus, where on a pet day we parked
at the end of the road, high over the sea,
you sat out in a folding chair, you the walker,

who in your health had never bothered with drives,
or views, or nuisances like the binoculars
you now focused on distant islands. And then:

Well, this is just paradise. I flinched away,
afraid your words would beat with huge, black wings
against the fragile day. But when I turned,

your wasting face was radiantly matter of fact
and that discordant irony I feared
was echoing only inside my humbled mind.

I remake that day now, and see it plain,
rinsed clear of all ironies, see you
fold up in your chair and walk, into wholeness.

Hayden Murphy

Two Elegies

Over the Rainbow

I. M. Thomas Corcoran
1 August 1906 - 8 November 1995

Light pierces through November haar.
Seen as phantom shapes, memories parade.
Half-seen Aislings, half-heard prayers.

In the West of Ireland languages sough
Into mulch-branched building of nests
By birds using watered earth to underline
Homes as carpeted shrines for those

Who then
Fly over the rainbow.

The palest of colour reflects on the relic
Bones wintering in memory.
Commemorating life singing with wind songs.

Beyond celebration.

Beneath the Sun

I. M. Bridget Corcoran
12 February 1912 - 20 April 1998

Heat arises to greet Spring
Thawing lakes and rivers round
The Holy Well. There lives a hymning chorus.

Outside Wexford lies a hill, cross
Named *Vinegar,* or, softer sighing,
Places of Martyrs. It overlooks
On clear-dawn days a tomb.

A hearth warm from fires, wood
Crossed with love.

In processional water ripples start,
Spread like memory, Bird
Choirs peal. Rainbow's miracle reflecting

Beneath the sun.

The Strange Case of the Vibrating Woman
Bernard MacLaverty

Your man's wife was out the messages when she felt a severe bite very near her nuptials. She was by the banana counter at the time and the very thought of a tarantula in her drawers nearly drove her daft. But the stinging was desperate. Anyway she got home and told your man about it and asked him to have a look – it being non-viewable. So it was drop the jeans and bend over time. He crouched looking up at her. There was a red area the size of an aubergine just below her right cheek.

"Inflamed," says your man. "Like myself."

That night your woman had switched on the blanket ready for going to bed. Your man always sits up late, drinking and watching the Open University – Periodic Classification, the elasticity of spun yarn, viscous flow through pipes and what have you. The next day he retains very little of it, not because of any shortcomings in the teaching, but because of the drink.

Anyway your woman wants to know if the swelling has gone down so she calls him to have a look. She's half-dressed, lying on the bed, knees to the chin.

"It's gone down a bit," he says. Then he reached out and touched the place. "Jesus, it's vibrating. I swear to God your bite is vibrating." Your woman straightens out, crosses her arms on her chest and prepares to die. Your man rests his hand on her waist. Then pulls it away as if HE is stung. "You're vibrating all over."

She cannot understand. She looks concerned and confused. She rests her own hand on her stomach but can feel nothing.

"You're having me on," she says.

"I'm not – honest, I'm not. You're going like a tuning fork." To prove his point he calls for the daughter. She arrives from her bedroom and puts her hand on her mother's stomach.

"Not that way," says your man. "With your finger tips – just touching and no more." The daughter gently touches her mother's stomach.

"Oh my God," she says. "Mum – he's right. You're vibrating." She laughs out loud but it is a serious kind of a laugh. "Maybe phone the doctor?"

"You say it was near the bananas?"

"You can't phone the doctor and say you got stung near the bananas."

"I didn't feel anything crawling up my leg BEFORE the bite. Maybe whatever it was, was in my jeans since this morning . . . maybe it was half dead."

"Like yourself," says your man. "It wouldn't surprise me."

Now it is like a scene from the faith healers, with the father and the daughter doing the laying on of hands, just touching the mother, hoping she'll stop.

"It's like getting your fingertips licked by a cat's tongue," said the daughter.

"Or the tingle you get from a drum."

"I don't know what you're talking about," says your woman. "And me lying here with my arms crossed like Deirdre from Airdrie."

Your man is still trying to describe the sensation. "It's like the hum I get off my reading light."

"Huh!" says your woman. "When did you ever do any reading?"

"Maybe it IS electric," says your man. He feels the scientist in himself taking over. All that late night viewing has not been wasted. In a moment of inspiration – equivalent to Newton making an apple tart or Archimedes mopping the bathroom floor – your man switches off the electric blanket.

Your woman becomes as still as a mill pond. The daughter confirms it.

"Keep your fingertips on her," says your man and switches on the blanket.

"She's going again," yells the daughter.

"Proof positive," he says and switches the wife off. "The question is, is it all of us? Or only those who have been bitten near the bananas?" The daughter lies down on the bed and the electric blanket is switched on.

Lo – she vibrates. Your man climbs on the bed and lo – the daughter gets his vibes through her fingertips.

Conclusion. Human beings, when they lie on electric blankets which are switched on, whether or not they have recently sustained a serious insect bite, vibrate like bowls of jelly sitting on a washing machine going at fast spin.

The Organiser

Bernard MacLaverty

Your man's friend, the painter, had had all sorts of praised heaped upon him. The only things he lacked were money and status. If only he'd had an OBE or some important honour heaped upon him. In order that this might come his way, he decided to do some work for Charity – organise a few fund-raising events. So he got on the phone to an old school chum – now a famous barrister.

"This is your old friend the painter," he said. "I was just trying to organise an event for a good cause and your name kept coming up . . ."

"That's nice."

"Friends kept mentioning you. Our causes are all good ones – Cancer, AIDS, Mental Illness, you know the kind of thing."

"Sounds very laudable. One could get an OBE out of that, if one was not careful."

"Yes. So we thought of a pinstripe bazaar."

"Sounds interesting. How exactly would it work?"

"Well, we haven't ironed out all the practical wrinkles yet, but it would probably go something like this. It takes me about a month, on average, to complete a painting – so we thought you could waive your fee for a month's work. The clients could pay the money direct to the charity we nominate."

"I'm sorry . . . "

"If it is a legal aid case then we could ask the State to pay directly to us, OR if that was too difficult maybe you . . ."

"I'm not fully understanding you. You want me to work for a month and give my wages to charity?"

"Yes – if you want to put it that way . . . You'll not be the only one, of course – we've decided to ask bank managers, share dealers, captains of industry, high flying accountants, the odd important surgeon – in the past they used to ask people like myself to donate a painting but this is chicken-feed compared to what you guys earn. It's hardly worth the effort of putting the red sticker on. As a barrister . . . "

"Are you a practical joker?"

"No – I'm serious. In my case it would be like asking for ONE measly painting . . ."

There was a click as the barrister put the phone down.

An Introduction to Publishing in Ireland

Hayden Murphy

Once upon a time, and a very good time and notion it was, the ambition of all and every emerging (from under the Icarus/Dedalus shadow of Yeats/Joyce) Irish writer was to be published by Liam Miller's Dolmen Press (1951-1987). Many were, including fourteen of the contributors to this issue of *Chapman*. Seamus Heaney was not. This is not to denigrate but rather to take a chance swipe at atonement. The decision to reject Heaney in 1965 was Miller's alone. I have been in error in suggesting Thomas Kinsella (who was advising editor to Dolmen) in other publications was involved. I am grateful to Thomas Kinsella for his verification of this fact in a letter of 11 July 1998.

Though never replaced as High Alter of font and testament Dolmen has begot many chapels, even begetters. I move geographically from the politically partitioned North to South. Blackstaff Press, child of the truly great Anne Tannahill, is the articulate and consistent voice of Belfast, ever alive to emerging sounds, drums and bells and echoes. Its championship of the shamefully ignored poets John Hewitt and Padraic Fiacc is but the sun-blessed tip of the literary iceberg. Metaphors sometimes sound hollow in the city that launched the Titanic. New lifeboats are launched by Laggan Press though its promotional skills are in a Byzantine fashion submerged. More amenable to the phone/fax is the Abbey Press (Editor, Adrian Rice). Beautiful presentation, competitive pricing, sensibly compression, the most welcome newcomer of the 90s.

Down in Dublin brave survivors ensure that the word goes out. Gallery Press (Editor, Peter Fallon) has since 1970 led the way. Writers in this issue published under its imprint include Pearse Hutchinson, Peter Sirr and Michael Hartnett. Since 1985 Dedalus Press (Editor, John F Deane) has built up a formidable backlist of voices enunciating the new. Among *Chapman* contributors are Hugh Maxton, Eva Bourke and Macdara Woods. It is also the printer/distributor of Thomas Kinsella's Peppercanister publications (see his essay). Over the years its authors have also inspired some memorable covers from John Behan RHA. Attic Press (Editor, Roisin Conroy), with a small staff, has over the last decade produced a remarkable file of evidence on new women's writing in Ireland. Particularly recommended are the works of Nell McCafferty introduced by Eavan Boland. Hugh Maxton appears as critic W J McCormac in Lilliput Press (Editor, Antony Farrell). Founded in 1985 it has an amazing range of titles gyrating from Flann O'Brien's adaptation (loosely, very loosely) of Capek's *The Insect* as *Rhapsody in Stephen's Green* to the intrinsically boring, but incidentally fascinating, history of Trinity College's *The Hist and Edmund Burke's Club* (£30) edited by Declan Budd and Ross Hinds (both Farrell, and long, long ago this writer, aged their youth in Trinity). Another mould breaking, and much recommended title is Dorothy Walker's *Modern Art in Ireland* (£25) with an introduction by Seamus Heaney.

Complementary, and indeed supplementary to this, is Theo Snoddy's *Dictionary of Irish Artists: 20th Century* (£50) from Seamus Cashmann's long established Wolfhound Press. In that house too you will find the many publications of the unbelievably forgotten Liam O'Flaherty.

Once based in Galway, now subsumed into Poolbeg, is the admirable Salmon Poetry (Editor, Jessie Lendennie). Among those in book form, whom you will read elsewhere in this edition, are Eithne Strong and Fred Johnston.

In Gaelic Coisceim and Clo Iar-Chonnachta will give you an in depth opportunity to find more of Seán Hutton and Gabriel Fitzmaurice.

I hope you would pursue to Cork University Press to get Patrick Galvin's *New and Selected Poems* (£9.95).

A Few Useful Addresses
Abbey Press: Courtenay Hill, Newry, Co Down BT34 3ED
Blackstaff Press: 3 Galway Park, Dundonald, Belfast BT16 0AN
Attic Press: 29 Upper Mount St., Dublin 2
Dedalus Press: 24 The Heath, Cypress Downs, Dublin 6W
Gallery Press: Loughcrew, Oldcastle, Co Meath
Poetry Ireland: Bermingham Tower, Dublin Castle, Dublin 2
Wolfhound: 68 Mountjoy Squre, Dublin 1
Cork University Press: University College, Cork
Salmon Poetry: Poolbeg Press, Knocksedan House, 123 Baldoyle Industrial Estate, Baldoyle, Dublin 13
Clo Iar-Chonnachtan: Indreabhan, Connemara, Co na Gaillimhe
Coisceim: Cosanic Teo, 127 Bothar na Tra, Dumach Tra, Balle Atha Cliath

Power Tools

Suzanne Thomson

The rottweiler crashed against the chain-link fence in a practised manoeuvre, bellowing its familiar warning.

"I prefer *cats*", Anita hissed in a stage whisper.

"What?" Guy called from the step ladder.

"What are you doing, Guy?"

"What the hell does it look like? Shut *up*," he said to the dog. "Christ. Why can't you two get along?" He fitted a large screw into the top of an iron bar over the face of the window. He pushed down with the screwdriver. The bar slipped and the screw popped out and fell to the hard-packed earth of the dog's mindless pacing.

"Well, why don't you come and help instead of just standing there staring?"

"He'll bite me."

"He will not. You're such a god-damned mouse."

Cerberus at the gate. Anita caught the inside of her cheeks in her teeth and lifted the glaring metal latch. Baked in the sun, the faeces-covered yard stank. She stepped in. Immediately the dog was there. She watched her own trembling fingers pull the latch over the post. Hot steamy breath wet Anita's thigh. The dog stood in her way. Saliva dripped on her bare toes. Without looking down, she took one step, brushing the dog's hot coat, then another. The dog gave way slightly and followed, stiff-legged, hair roached along its spine. She tasted blood.

"Get *down*, Buster." Guy hoisted the iron bar back up. "Just hold it there. Don't let it move."

"But we don't need bars."

"Are you kidding? Ernie says the house two doors down from his got robbed last week."

"Ernie."

He twisted in the last screw, then looked at her clothes – her only decent pair of shorts and sandals. "Where are you going?"

"To the theatre. We're going to start building the set this weekend."

"Well, you'll have to walk. I need the truck later."

She went to the gate, the dog closer than her shadow. She slid through and pulled it shut quickly, in a panic that the dog would push out after her. The gate pinched the dog's muzzle. It yipped and shook its head. A string of white saliva landed on her shin. Anita was elated.

"Hey! What'd you do to him?"

"He stuck his nose in the gate. Guy, what are we going to do about Buster when a baby comes?"

Guy closed his eyes and exhaled sharply. "What did we agree?"

She couldn't stop herself, the words like tiny bubbles on the swell of her impulse. "You wouldn't have to do anything. I'd take care of it. I'd do everything. I want a baby more than . . ."

"We're not going to talk about it. I'm busy."

Anita turned to go. It was all too precarious, and she no longer trusted her instincts.

"What is it this time?" he shouted.

She stopped. "What?"

"The play."

"*The Tempest*." She started to walk away, then stopped and said, "Shakespeare." Then to herself, "I shouldn't have said that, I shouldn't have said that."

But Guy only shook his head and balanced the screwdriver on the top of the ladder and climbed down. "Shakespeare." He took the dog's broad black head in his hands and rumpled its ears and pulled its head back and forth. "You're my baby, yes you are." He kissed its brow and rubbed his face against it. "You're Daddy's Busty-wusty baby."

She moved slowly through the heat as if through thick water. Once in the hundreds, the hot air became a new element, demanding caution. Anita took slow breaths through her mouth, as the air passing through her nostrils made them burn. The roofs of the buildings could not coalesce. Cars passed with sticky sounds as their tires pulled melted tar from jig-saw cracks in the road.

Approaching the playhouse she did not hurry but kept a measured pace all the way to the double-doored entrance and stepped into air-conditioned darkness. She stood for a moment, blinded, and felt the sweat go cool on her skin. Then past the carpeted foyer, under grotesque masks of tragedy and comedy, beyond the door into the theatre proper, down the long sloping aisle with burgundy coloured seats on either side. She skipped a couple of steps with the downward momentum, and stopped at the abrupt lip of the stage. Peter, the director, was bent over on the stage, one knee on a stud, both hands gripping an electric drill.

"Hey, Anita," he called. "Just in time. Come hold this steady, would you?"

Rather than going up the steps on either side of the stage, she hoisted herself up where she stood, and went to him and grasped the stud in both hands. Peter pushed the bit through the wood, sinking it in and pulling it back a few times to get a clean hole.

"We need to use as much scrap as possible. I'm going to try," he stood and surveyed the stage, "to build a ship's deck – just a suggestion – downstage. With ropes and maybe a railing and just the shape of the bow, with a pretty steep slant. If we can make it so that we can push the whole thing into the wings, that would be perfect."

Anita already saw it. Cool air filled her lungs. "If the ropes and a little scaffolding could be rigged to the cat-walk, dropped down and lashed to a mobile deck . . . that pawn-shop on Main Street has an old wheel, a ship's wheel. Maybe they'd let us borrow it if we mention them in the programme."

He pulled the trigger on the drill to spin it. "How would you like to be stage manager for this production?"

"Really? I'd love to!" She thought of Guy's reaction. "Oh, but, I don't know." She thought of the dog. "Well . . ." And of Ernie. "Yes. Yes, I will. I'd do a good job. I wouldn't let you down."

He picked up the wood and dragged it upstage to lean it against a stack of old flats. "I know. That's why I asked you. Have you ever used a power saw? Come on. Once you get used to it, there's no going back."

Guy turned from her and took something from the top drawer.

"Oh, Guy, no. Please."

He fumbled it onto himself, slender hips thrust forward. "Turn on your stomach", he said.

"Guy," she groaned. "Take it off. I want a baby. A baby. My own baby."

"Well, I don't." He pushed her knees apart and knelt between them.

In the darkness outside the bedroom window, now securely barred, the dog paced, growling. Its stink permeated the house, despite the cleaning she'd done that same morning, pushing the stringy head of the mop back and forth across the kitchen floor with one listless hand. The other clutched the script of *The Tempest*, and she read while she mopped, eyes darting side to side. Magical phrases leapt out, drawing gasps of pleasure. Some lines began to return of their own volition at appropriate moments.

As now.

Misery acquaints a man with strange bedfellows.

"I *do* love you," Guy said to the back of her head. "I *do*." And then, "Oh, oh great. Great."

"Never mind," she said.

Later, at ten-thirty, the doorbell rang. Guy switched off the television with the remote and jumped out of bed. He pulled on a pair of jeans. Anita heard his joyful voice as he lead Ernie into the kitchen for a beer, then into the den. She got up to shut the bedroom door, then climbed back into bed. She pulled the covers over her head and rolled into a ball, stifling the strange sound in her constricted throat by forcing her thoughts to the building of Prospero's cell with the scraps of lumber.

The circular saw was too frightening, too powerful and heavy, but the saber saw could do most of the work. The ship's deck needed another brace behind and below. During the blocking of the scene, the wild stumbling and heaving on the ropes by the mariners had suddenly ceased when the deck tilted under their weight, and Anita was called in to find a solution.

"Heigh, my hearts!" she said to the buzzing blade slowly etching through the two-by-four. "Cheerly, cheerly, my hearts! Yare, yare!"

The end of the stud clanked to the floor. The sharp retort pleased her, and she swaggered a little as she stood, saber saw in hand, carpenter's belt girding her hips. She mounted the deck and pulled on a rope and imagined the waves beneath. She rocked back and forth, eyes dim in the sea dream.

In the silence, a rich baritone filled the theatre. One of the actors, the man who played Ferdinand.

"I kissed her once and I kissed her twice, and we were wond'rous merry!"

She looked over her shoulder. He stood half-way down the aisle, arms folded. He was singing to her.

"Hasn't Patty said anything about how much time he spends here?" Anita asked from the kitchen sink.

"Why should she?" Guy said. "Is there something weird about a couple of friends hanging out? Do I say anything about how much time you spend at the theatre? Do I?"

"No." It was true. She didn't know what to think of that.

"If you ask me, it's a lot more than I spend with Ernie. But do you hear me complaining? If that's what you want to do", he found the remote and fell into his chair, "then do it."

She scrubbed in puzzled wonder, hardly aware of the dry layer of mashed potato on the plate. The dog, listening for sounds from the kitchen window, crashed against the outside wall and yodelled. Anita dropped the dish and it broke in two.

"A pox o' your throat, you bawling, blasphemous, incharitable dog!"

Guy turned from the television. "*What* did you say?"

How many goodly creatures are there here! Anita thought as she watched Ferdinand and the others, but particularly Ferdinand. How beauteous mankind is!

"Stop, stop, stop," Peter yelled. "Anita, where are the logs?"

She sidled between the flats and came on stage, hands to her face. "Oh, my God."

"Dress rehearsal is in three days," Peter said. "Three days! Can you please please have them here tomorrow?"

"I will, I promise." She ran backstage and returned with lumber scraps. "Here", she thrust them at Ferdinand. "Use these tonight."

He made as if to lift them from her arms, but before taking them, bent and craned his head and kissed her astonished mouth.

"Wrong wench, Ferdinand! Stephano, give us your last line, let's try this again, and let's get through it this time with no interruptions."

"What the hell are you doing now?"

"The sheets are dirty again." Anita looked in wonder at the crumpled, stained linen. "I'm going to strip the bed."

"What is it with you?" Guy demanded. "You're obsessed with washing the damned sheets. Aren't you supposed to be gone? Isn't this opening night? So leave."

The sound of the refrigerator closing, and the clink of two beer bottles came from the kitchen.

Anita steadied herself against the door frame. "Yes. All right."

When she stepped into the hot night, she heard a key enter the lock behind her and the latch bolt slide into its well-lubricated strike.

She made a slight detour and rang Patty's doorbell.

"Hi Anita! Ernie's already tried to get me to join you, but he knows I don't like to play cards."

"I work at the playhouse, Patty. The community theatre. I work there every night."

Patty's mask of sociable bonhomie slowly sloughed off. "You don't play cards." She suddenly looked weary.

"Here are my house keys." Anita held them up. "I'm on my way to the theatre. I may not come back. If you want to know, go into the house. Go to our bedroom. Here's the bedroom key, in case. Then you'll know for sure. If you want to know."

Even though she was late, Anita hid behind a van parked across the street and watched her own home.

"But release me from my bands," she said softly, "with the help of your good hands."

Patty appeared, a wraith gliding across the feeble, dry lawn. She opened the door without a sound, the dead bolt and the handle lock, and went into the silent house.

A light came on at the side, their bedroom, and then a woman's scream. Men cursed, their coupled silhouette against the thin curtain and bars. The dog set up a snorting, choking, howling racket.

"Now my charms are all o'erthrown," Prospero said to the lighting room above the heads of the audience, "and what strength I have's mine own, which is most faint."

Backstage, Ferdinand's breath was sweet on her neck. "You've enchanted me, my dark clever sylph." His lips brushed her tingling ear.

Anita smelled his make-up. She started to laugh, thinking of the better drama unfolding at her home, and pressed her mouth shut against it. Her gaze was frank and open. "I want to have fun. Let's go to the cast party, then dancing somewhere. I don't want to go home tonight."

He drew back a little. "My little pixie blossoms quickly."

"As you from crimes would pardoned be," intoned Prospero, "let your indulgence set me free." Applause rippled then burgeoned, blending with the roar of late summer rain pounding the tin roof over the loading dock at the back of the theatre.

"This is a good production," said Anita.

"We all play our parts well. Meet me here, in twenty minutes?" Ferdinand touched her cheek with his finger and left to join the others for many bows behind the falling and rising and falling curtain.

The cordless drill easily twirled out the screws. They fell into the chrysanthemums growing over the dog's former path of fury. Anita left them there, below yellow flowers just opening to the cool of autumn.

The chain-link was removed and Anita had build a picket fence in its place. She propped open the new wooden gate and collected the bundle of iron bars and carried them around the house to the garage, then returned with a four-by-four to begin work on a little deck.

The circular saw Peter lent her held no terrors now. It made clean, quick cuts precisely where she wanted them.

"Pretty neat", said a voice in the sudden silence after the blade stopped spinning. It was the man who had played Ferdinand in *The Tempest*.

"Hi." Anita brushed her hair back with a gloved fist.

"A little sprite like you doing all this building."

"With power tools," she said, "you can do anything."

"So it seems. I was wondering if you'd like to have dinner. That new restaurant." He leaned against the gate and kicked at the wisps of grass around its clean post.

She hitched up her carpenter's belt. The hammer's handle dangling from its leather loop slapped happily against her thigh. "And what's happened to Leslie?"

Leslie had played Miranda.

He shrugged.

"You can't just drop a slyph and expect her to fly back when you want her again." She smiled at him without malice.

"So, no?"

"No. But thanks."

"Oh well", he straightened but kept his hands on the points of the pickets. "Looks like you have what you want."

"And what I don't have," Anita said, "I make."

"See you 'round, maybe at try-outs?"

"You're a sweetheart," she called after him.

He shook his head as he left.

A battered theatre copy of *The Crucible* lay on the small table by the front door and on it a postcard from San Francisco. Guy and Ernie had found an apartment that took dogs and were very happy in their brave new world, though if Anita could talk to Patty and suggest she be as reasonable as Anita had been regarding lawyer's fees and settlements, they'd be grateful.

She shooed the kitten from the chair and sat down to read the script, letting her imagination wander to costumes and props. The house smelled of fresh paint and new curtains and scented geraniums.

Anita had been aware while she read of what felt like a muscle twitching in her abdomen. In an instant her eyes went wide and the script dropped to her lap. Her hands moved under her sweatshirt to the smooth skin of her belly, and they felt it, too.

The quickening.

"Spirit", Anita whispered, "which by mine art I have from your confines called to enact my present fancies, welcome!"

The kitten jumped up to settle on her lap, until drops of water hit the downy gray fur of its body. It shook its head and leaped off, then turned an ear to the steady ticking of tears on the script.

Lesson

Jim McLaughlin

Miss Devine waits for the stillness to fall. The children are expectant, faces turned to her in anticipation. Miss Devine looks up, conducting the silence with her raised hands, knowing the pause will add to their excitement, give rush and flow to their words. They sit with their hands clasped tight in an attitude of prayer.

Miss Devine looks down and sees that Mairead appears to be just as absorbed as the other children. The girl is wearing pigtails that are plaited slightly askew giving an abstracted look to her small, round features. But her eyes are intent and Miss Devine is pleased at the sight of the pudgy, little fingers, knitted together in front of her lips, as if she is trying to breath warmth into them in spite of the sunlight flashing through the blinds on the windows. Miss Devine is reassured. She begins. "And what do you have there, Michael?" Michael peeks into the cleft under his crossed thumbs and describes his secret friend. His language is articulate and clear and Miss Devine is satisfied with her choice. Michael tells her how he met the angel and what he looks like, how the angel helps him and how he can always talk to his angel when he is feeling lonely.

After the initial rush of words Michael hesitates, groping for an idea and Miss Devine holds up a warning finger, sustaining the necessary quiet in the room. She quickly glances across the class, taking note of the joined hands thrust devotionally upward, relishing the little gasps of longing. Only then does she give the required utterance of approval, helping Michael find new inspiration. She savours the surprise revealed in the child's eyes as he discovers himself creating in response to her words.

The children begin to swing forward under her fluid orchestration. There are pauses, of course, little breathing spaces and missed beats when they almost slip away from her but she can feel the pulse of the lesson, knows what is needed. She uses the spaces of silence, allows time for ideas to swell, to gather impetus and come surging to her again.

The children laugh at the descriptions of tiny dogs and butterflies that send out signals with rainbow wings. Miss Devine echoes their amusement. They groan in fascinated repulsion when Declan tells them that his friend is a slippery, slithery rat, living in the gutter above his bedroom window. Miss Devine contrives a face and tells Declan to make sure to keep his hands tightly shut until his friend leaves. Declan grins proudly and shakes his closed hands at the girl sitting next to him. She twists away and the others laugh.

Miss Devine is a rock and their thoughts come splashing over and around her. She is magnetic, attractive to their minds, gathering all she desires from the tide, holding it, shaping it, directing the flow of excited energy back to the children. She glides through the room, reaping the waves of imagination, drawing what she wants and needs from them. She is in control, creating structures in the air of the room.

When little Elaine tells Miss Devine that the friend she is clutching so tightly to her stomach is her Granma Lena who died the children fall into an enthralled hush. Miss Devine can feel them waiting on her to hold everything together, to put it right. She moves towards the little girl, quick to display the essential compassion. She says that Elaine has a friend who will always look after her. Elaine's chin has dropped and Miss Devine kneels beside her. She gives Elaine a hug and tells her that her friend is someone who really loves her and that her friend wants her to be happy and smile, doesn't she? Elaine nods and Miss Devine lifts the little chin up with her finger. Elaine looks up to her and shakes away the tears.

She is aware now that it is time to consolidate and move on. She shifts quickly to the board at the top of the room. Elaine has unexpectedly provided her with a cue for she wants to talk to the children about how much real friends give to us.

"We have great fun with our secret imaginary friends," she says, "but we show love to our real friends." And she smiles down at Elaine. She is always a comfort to her children. The little girl smiles back happily.

"Isn't that true." The class agree.

"And what do our real friends do for us?"

Fingers wave in the warm air and Miss Devine scans the room for someone who has not had the chance to speak. Her fingers dance over the children's heads. For a moment she fastens on Mairead but sees that her hand is not up. Her hands are still clutched together under her chin. As usual she is two steps behind and now the pout is on her lips. Miss Devine moves past her and calls on Ryan.

"They play with us, Miss."

"Yes, they do, don't they, Ryan."

And Miss Devine begins to write on the board in large, elegant letters. Other children raise their hands, reach high, urgent to vouch the plain truthes that Miss Devine wishes to affirm. The words are laid down on the board, clear for them all to see and remember, direct as commandments.

Friends help each other.

Friends listen to each other.

Friends share.

Friends show love to one another.

Miss Devine is keen to get the class started on the work she has planned to reinforce all that has been said. Some still want to talk but their thoughts and concentration are focused now and it is time to engage them in purposeful activity in order to fulfil her objectives for the lesson – time to turn ideas into action, abstract thought into concrete artefacts.

Miss Devine reads back what is written and tells the children that she is sure they can make some things that would show the love they have for their friends. She swings around the board, ready, her skirt swirling. She is conscious of her imposing presence. She has them. They are attentive. They are prepared to work hard for her. The children are waiting on her word. But there she is, the skewed pigtails, the staring eyes, the hands joined beneath the round face, the pouted lips.

Miss Devine is pleased with how she has constructed the lesson. She looks over the class with relish, gratified at the discipline she has instilled in these children, how they are patient with each other, attentive and responsive to her. She will give Mairead her chance quickly before they move on though, God knows, it is difficult enough to get her to talk when you want her to say something. But she will not allow Mairead to distract her sense of clarity and purpose. She will not allow the structure she has created to be disrupted.

"Well then, Mairead, do you have something to tell us?"

Mairead smiles widely showing the gap where two front teeth have disappeared. "I have a friend, Miss."

She holds up her hands, one locked tightly into the other. Miss Devine gives her the grave look and some of the children in front look around at her.

"You know we're talking about our real friends now, don't you, Mairead? Is this a real friend you're talking about?"

"Yes, Miss."

Miss Devine purses her lips and raises her eyebrows and rolls a look around the class and back to Mairead. Declan sniggers but cuts it off as Miss Devine's finger lifts.

"Well, Mairead," she breathes, "and what do you call this friend of yours?"

"Solissa, Miss."

"Sleesamess?" Miss Devine is sorry for this. She is intrigued by the name but she wants to finish this quickly.

"No . . . Solissa – that's her name, Miss."

"Oh, and where is this friend of yours, then, Mairead? Can we meet her?"

Mairead pushes her hands out. "Here she is, Miss."

Miss Devine is patient because the girl seems to be deadly serious. There is always one. She resigns herself to ending it but as soon as possible. "And are you going to let us see Solissa, Mairead? She's real, is she?"

"Yes, Miss."

"You're holding her very tightly, you know, she can't be very comfortable in there. I'm sure it's extremely hot..."

Declan and Ryan laugh. Miss Devine shoots them the quick and cold shut up look and quickly turns her full attention back to Mairead. The pigtails have not budged. Miss Devine knows the girl is not acting. The hands are still knotted together, reluctant to part.

"What is your friend like, Mairead?" Miss Devine says, softly.

Mairead looks up, grinning. "She's like a tear, Miss."

"Like a tear?" She says surprised. "Like a tear from your eye?"

"Yes, Miss."

"Where did she come from, Mairead?"

"I made her."

"You made her – isn't that wonderful. And how did you do that?"

The word 'secret' is lisped between the gap in her teeth – "It's a seeked, Miss."

Miss Devine cannot keep this monosyllabic inquisition up much longer. More of the children laugh this time but she knows it is not fair to be hard on them because they have been so good. "It's a secret? Well real people usually aren't secrets, Mairead."

The little girl stares down at her hands. Miss Devine can almost feel her thoughts moving. The pigtails come up again, pointing to heaven and earth at the same time.

"Miss, I caught my tear in one hand and caught the light coming in the window in the other and then I rubbed them together until they were all mixed up and then I made the magic breath and Solissa was there."

All of the children are listening now. Miss Devine is trying hard to conceal her irritation. She is going to have to work hard to refocus their attention on the work ahead. "And do you talk to Solissa, Mairead?"

Mairead looks up at Miss Devine with her head cocked, the pigtails turning in new angles, as if this were an absurd question. "Yes, Miss," she says righteously, almost indignant.

Miss Devine chews hard on the inside of her cheek. She performs a quick mental scrutiny of Mairead's parents and makes her judgement against them. These films, they disturbed children's thoughts. People should be more aware. "Well, Mairead, do you think if you asked Solissa to go for a wee while – so that you could use your hands to work – do you think she would do that for you?"

Miss Devine is determined that 'Solissa' will because she will make her, irrespective of what 'Solissa' wants.

"Yes, Miss."

Miss Devine is relieved that she does not have to demonstrate her authority to the class. Mairead opens out her hands, palms up, and gives an almost imperceptible push upwards. Miss Devine claps her hands in a show of glee and cries out, pointing towards the large open window.

"Oh, look, there she goes now."

She dances over to the window where the blinds flutter lightly in the breeze and shades her eyes with her hand. "Isn't she beautiful?"

She does not notice that the children are not looking. All their eyes are following the little iridescent tear of light as it gleams across the board, dances for a flickering moment amongst the notes of chalk dust floating in a sunbeam and flashes suddenly through the keyhole.

"Miss Devine?" Declan raises his hand uncertainly.

Miss Devine turns and motions Declan to put his hand down.

"But, Miss . . . "

He is supplicant.

"Not now, Declan dear," says Miss Devine. "We really must get started on our real work." Miss Devine opens her arms out, reclaiming the devotion of her class.

Hands

Peter Cameron

It's mony a lang day syne, thon braw simmer day in the fouth o the year. Lang syne, and mair clear nou nor aa the trauchles o yestreen.

It was yae day in the saicont year o the War, aye, the muckle war, no the wee ane wi Stalingrad and El Alamein and sic cangles in the schuil playgrund.

Me and my butties used to gang owre by the auld pit where the men had been drouned, and reid watter cam frae ablow the grund. Gin you pit your hand in, it wasna cauld, like watter frae the hill, aa clear dews and a hunder year o rain on the heich stanes.

The reid watter had nae cauld on it, it cam frae a place where nae snaw flew, wi a smell o ablow the grund, o carbide and cauld afore the green warld was made, and God garred his sons howk the grund for coal.

Whiles I would gang mysel, aiblins on a winter's day, wi the reid abune in the lift burnin wi hurts and skaiths a laddie canna ken. Then, the burn was reid wi a wearisome wabbit reid, the colour o a dune man's bluid.

I would hunker doun, and vizzy in the tunnel as far in ablow the hill as I could see, and furder nor that wi a bairn's ee, intil the mirk hert o the pit, where the heid-banes o the deid miners chappit thegither like wet dominoes and the watter gaed throu them, year on year.

Whatsomever was in the burn, it made the bank rowthie and rank wi dockens, and a sugarally smell o fennel, and the wild ingan.

I cam wi Wullie this day, caller in a simmer's morn, and there ablow was the burn, in its bed o pink glaur.

What was that like a chuckie-stane, juist ablow the runnel o the rinnin watter? Wullie pit his hand in the reid watter and furth it cam.

I couldna for the life o me tell what it was. The white brainch o a tree? A bit cuist ferm graith?

The nackie bane o a man's hand was in Wullie's hand, aye thegither.

He kent what it was, afore I did. He held it ablow the watter, and the reid glaur atween the knuckle banes laved awa. A man's hand.

I felt a het cramp in my leg, and a goloch or a flee souked at the swyte on my brou. A dirl cam fornent my ain banes at the ugsome, ferlie thing, yon byous bane.

A picture o his daith in the mirk cam intil my mind, and the muckle stane on his breist as it waited a wee, and shiftit aince mair, and waited a wee, and shiftit aince mair, and ilka bruckle bane o his kist crackt, and brak, and ranced the bluidy hert like a airn maig.

And aa the folk gaun about the houss, the scones on the table and the whisky catchin the licht on the aumry the afternune o his kistin. Nae bed-rel, nae liggin in the parlour while you get ready for the saft mirk o the grund. And in the nicht, the last outby the grave, the nock chappin the nicht hours, and a sabbin greet frae the shut bed ben the houss.

And the daw cam, and the grave howked juist perjink, wi the glisk o cley, and the meenister festenin his sark stud, the word o your deid sermon comin til his mind.

No for you, my lad. Nae Hell nor bedrel, juist the mirk ablow the grund, and eternity about you like a mortclaith.

Aye, ablow the grund, in the ae mirk, and nane for company but the heid-bane o your butty.

Thae thochts that gang throu your mind, a laddie, and nane but a denty bit bane to pit them there – that and the thocht o your ain daith on you and the tree abune you, a rowan wi the simmer scent on it, hertsome sweet and sherp as daith, and the reid burn ablow, like auld dune bluid.

At aince, Wullie flang the hand-bane frae him, back intil the mirk ablow the bing, and aff he gaed rinnin, athort the green corn. We baith ran as fast and as far as life itsel; nae daith could snare or catch us in his bany neive, and as I ran, I grat for the deid man and the bonny bane o his hand, I grat for mysel, and the bluid sang in my heid, and I was livin aye, in the warld and young.

When I cam til mysel, it was like a dwam, and I was my lane. In my neb was the smell o rowan, and the smell o roustit airn, that birls in your heid like a peerie.

Comin throu the door, I banged intil my Grannie, here frae the ferm.

'Weel, Doddie,' quo she, 'your new titty sleeps on the bowster aside your Mither. Dicht that clart frae your knees and gie your face and hands a lave.'

The parlour was half-mirk, and there was a smell o talcum pouther and ablow that, the birth-smell o a bairn.

The bairn ligged quaet on the bowster, tired frae her lang low road.

Her een were open, and she saw me by the door, and her first smell o rowan on me and the reid burn.

She was gaucy, yon bairn, and she lauched. She haud up her airm and the sterk sun, throu the blind, showed me the sweep o the rosy bane throu the split new flesh.

Yon bairn's deid, and I'm gey nearhand mysel.

The auld fern years, filled and stapped wi naething, juist life itsel. An auld man, namely for naething. I've dune naething wi my life.

The rowth o't 's in my mind. I never had saut til my kail or a jewel on my hand. There's a wee bittie, a paper pound or twa, in the kist aside the bed, and there's nane here kens my name. They caa me George, and my name's Dod.

I carena for ocht. I hae mysel aye, hert and mind, and aa the simmer and winter days.

The nurse comes round, white and blae. Och, aince mair for a neive o cauld snaw, aince mair the scent o rowan and the smell o the reid burn, comin furth frae the hill o eild and daith and me alive!

Falling Leaves

Eleanor Thomson

In October, leaves fall in the countryside. They lie in the fields like orange and yellow snowdrifts. Here, in Hope Street, there are no autumn colours. Just exhaust fumes gathering in damp grey corners. Only people fall here, like my best friend Maggie. They fall and lie in the gutter. Like dead leaves.

Glasgow's Hope Street points like a big crooked finger north. I'm standing in the darkness at the tip of that finger. I'm feeling sick and alone because, ten minutes ago, I watched Maggie fall into the gutter like a damp leaf. I know nothing can save her. She saw me watching her. She knows she's finished. A drunken slag at fifteen.

Maggie and me lived near each other until her ma died last month. She hasn't got a da or anybody so she's in a home now.

We often come into the city on Saturday afternoons, like today. We never have any money but we don't care. Sometimes Maggie can wangle money from people. Old folk chat to us on the bus sometimes. Maggie pretends to be shy and peeks at them from behind her long red hair. This is my sister, she lies, smiling.

"Hello, hen," they smile at us and nod. Then Maggie really winds them up. "Where's the Royal Infirmary, Missis? Are we on the right bus? We're visitin' our ma . . . ."

The old souls get worried, "You'll no get tae the Infirmary on this bus, hen . . ."

Maggie's a great actress. She turns to me, devastated, "Oh, *no* – we've nae mare money fur'r fare. We canny get anither bus . . .Whit'll we dae . . ?"

She can usually get up to a quid this way although I don't like doing these things. Maggie does a lot of things I don't really like. She's got no conscience, that Maggie. I should've known that she'd go too far one day.

Maggie's ma got drunk every day when she was alive. I can't remember seeing her standing, or walking, or ever doing anything except sitting in her big greasy armchair. Sometimes, when she wasn't too drunk to speak, she told us how much she hated her life. Maggie says her ma never got over her da leaving her. He hasn't been seen since Maggie was two.

But now her ma's dead. Died on Maggie's fifteenth birthday. Cheap wine and pills. Maggie came in from school and found her. Dead.

"I won't get like her," Maggie had said, "I'm no goin' to be a drunken slag like her."

Sometimes I think mothers aren't up to much. Ma left da and me a year ago, when I was fourteen. Went off with her fancy-man. Let us down. Let me down.

He was a big plonker, anyway, da said. The guy was dead soft. No backbone. "A big nancy-boy," da would say. Not like da at all. "Your da thinks he's the hard man o' the East End," ma used to say before she left.

"Ah don't know whit yer mither sees in him, hen," da would say to me when ma went away. It was horrible to see the hurt trapped in his eyes after she left us. He just sat in his armchair staring out of the window, picking his nose. Moody looking. Shrunk into himself. I used to feel dead sorry for him. Used to – before he started behaving like I was her.

He went into these moods. His whole face would change – red and screwed up. "Yer jist like her, y'know," he would shout. "Look at you – white faced wee bitch!" He would explode that last word through his lips and finish it with a sound at the back of his throat, like he was going to be sick. This went on for weeks. Maggie used to say to me, "Leave him to stew on his own". Come to my house. We'll look after each other.

Things got worse. He started bringing these women home. They would try to ignore me, "Get rid of her, Jim, will ye? Ah canny stand her eyes," or they would say, "Whit ur ye lookin' at? Can ye no' go oot an play or sumthin'?"

Their voices were dry, hacking with too many cigarettes, papery-sounding, like dead leaves in the wind. I hated them. I hated why they came to our house.

From where I'm standing in Hope Street, I can see Glasgow's Theatre Royal. All the rich folk from the countryside come to watch drama or ballet there. They come from places where autumn leaves fall and colour the streets. Nice places. People with posh accents live in these places. They say, "Bearsden" or "Newton Mearns" with their lips pursed, like they're chewing something nice. The places Maggie and me know sound more like curses at closing time.

Tonight, the Theatre Royal looks lovely. There's a glow from the main door. Inside, there's soft carpeting, shiny brass and crystal lighting. I like to look.

Right behind the Theatre, sprawling black in the dark, there's the Scottish Television buildings. Broadcasting masts bristle above, big twisted black shapes, high in the night sky. I think about the signals from these masts sending copies of films and shows and people all over Scotland. Wee bits of life, cut and dried and sugar coated, like candied ginger.

Television's boring to watch, but. I'd rather see the crowds going into the Theatre. Maggie likes the crowds, too. On days like today we always finish up hanging around the theatre. We pretend that we're going to see a play, standing around til all the people are inside. Once they go in, though, we feel a bit lost. It's then that we make up our own play. We're always two rich ladies who travel the world and have loads of clothes and jewellery and handsome men. Then we go to the chip shop and go home. We didn't tonight, but.

I used to like these nights when we went to her house before her ma died. Before Maggie had to go into the children's home. I felt safer away from da. We used to have a great laugh, me and Maggie. At bed time we would jam into her wee bed. We'd act daft. Shove each other out. Giggling at what someone had said to us or how they'd looked. The whole world seemed funny when we thought about it. I thought we'd be happy for ever. Friends for ever. We shared everything. Maggie and me. We told each other everything.

"Don't worry", she would say, "we'll look after each other. We're like sisters, you'n me. We'll always stick together. See yer crabbit auld da – forget him. Come an' stay here."

Sometimes, though, I didn't like staying at Maggie's. Sometimes she took too much of her ma's drink. I used to get frightened. People do silly things when they're drunk and Maggie's daft enough. She always wanted to dance and play loud music when she was drinking. Her ma never cared. She was always too drunk.

Once, a neighbour thumped on the door, "Come oot o' ther, ya hoors," came a man's voice, "Cut the noise or I'll break this door doon!"

I was scared but Maggie opened the door. She was still dancing, her feet moving like slow gymnastics, hips moving rhythmically, her hands behind her neck holding her hair away from her face. A big giant of a man stood there. Maggie looked up at him. "Hello, Mr. Wilson. Is it Ma yer wantin'? She's sleepin'." He opened his mouth to speak, his face twisted with temper. She had her back turned to me. I don't know what he saw in her eyes but he gave a wee smile and shuffled his feet, "Look, hen, jist turn the music doon a bit, eh?"

"Okay, Mister Wilson." Maggie closed the door in his face.

Just before she closed the door he had looked at her. Made me think of da, that look. All loose lipped and droopy eyed. "It's jist yer da, hen." He was coming in my bedroom door. Twelve o'clock at night. Me sitting up in my bed trying to finish my homework for Mrs. Patterson. An essay. "Jist fur a wee minute, hen. I'm awfy fed up. Why did yer ma leave us, hen." He choked on a sob. Came over to sit on my bed. Sitting there in his sweaty shirt and dirty old boxer shorts, not caring about the gap at the front of them. Gettin in beside me, "Jist fur a wee cuddle, hen." His breath. Boozy my ma would call it. Boozy Breath.

There's mirrors and glass on the front of the pub opposite the Theatre Royal. The mirrors are bright with reflected light. The pub doors are wafting open and closed. I can smell the sweet stench of booze, sweat and cheap perfume coming from the people drinking there. I listen to them; loud laughter, deep roars and screeching shouts of it.

Maggie went back in there a few minutes ago, after it happened, her long red hair hiding her face. She couldn't even look at me. I can't stop staring at these pub doors. I can't do anything. I feel so alone.

Maggie was going to get somewhere of her own, you know. She said when she left the children's home they would give her a flat if she wanted. She said we would live there. She said not to worry. We would look after each other. I believed her. I can see different things in her now, but . . .

The thing is, she knows. She knows nothing can save her, no matter what she used to say. I'll never get like them, she would say. Dirty slags. But it's what she's done that counts.

After all the theatre crowds had gone in, she said we should go to the pub instead of the chippy.

Then I said, "What about the folk in the Home? They'll no like it if you go back half cut."

She got really ratty with me. "Don't be such a big wean," she had shouted at me. "C'mon. We're goin' fur a drink. There's fuck-all else to do."

"I don't want a drink. What if we get caught?"

"Mary, you don't look like a wee lassie, you're just acting like one. Nobody'll know we're under eighteen."

"We've nae money, but . . ."

"So what? Somebody'll buy us one!"

We're inside the pub. I don't want a drink but I need to look after her. It's crowded in there – a big crowd from the football. They're really happy, drunk. We wait.

His voice is rough, his words slurred, his arm heavy round my shoulders as he sits next to me, too close.

"Aw, c'mon, hen." He gives me a wee squeeze.

"NO!"

Maggie's laughing loudly and being helped out of the pub by the other one. She's drunk. Five vodkas.

"Maggie, don't go . . ." She doesn't hear me.

"Och, ssh . . ." He puts a nicotine-brown finger to his lips for me to be quiet. "C'mon, hen, s'only a wee bit fun. Ther's yer sister away. D'ye no' like me or sumthin'?"

I look at him; sweaty, fat and ugly, wearing a football scarf. "Fuck off!"

I run outside, looking for Maggie. She's with him on the other side of the street, in the darkened doorway of an old church. He's taller than her, pushing close, standing a step below her, his back turned to the street. I cross the road. They don't see me. He's close; too close. Above his left shoulder I can see her head is thrown back, like she's looking at the twisted shapes of the broadcasting masts above the theatre. She lowers her eyes to street level.

She sees me watching and looks away. Her hair's the colour of autumn leaves; leaves that fall before the long winter.

Thirteen

Alan Long

The calendar hung on the wall. One date was circled – Friday, 13th. McGurk hauled the bed-clothes over his head and buried his face deep in the pillow, each centimetre blocking out more of the sunlight which filtered in through the curtains. He harboured no intentions of rising early today – in fact, no intention of rising at all. Today was Friday the 13th.

The bedroom door breezed open and his sister pranced in, crossing to the window and opening the curtains with all the ceremony of a child on Christmas morning. The light flooded the room and drowned McGurk. Now all was lost, all hope was gone – no chance of returning to his blissful state of unconsciousness. He emitted a groan, like that of a wild dolphin pursued by David Attenborough and a team of award-hungry cameramen.

"Can you no gie me peace wumman?" he barked at her, some of the impact and harshness of the words being lost by the muffling qualities of the pillow. "Dae ye no ken whit day it is?"

"Och, don't you start oan that Friday the thirteenth blarney. Is it no jist disgraceful? A seventy-year-auld man that wilnae get oot his bed cos o a load of superstitious nonsense. I suppose ye'll no be eating oanythin either?" His sister's words lost none of their harshness, although McGurk remained suitably unimpressed. He had heard it all before, and nothing was going to remove him from his bed, or vice versa.

"Ye know I'll no be eating. I dinnae want to be poisoned." McGurk surrendered to the fact that his attempts at slumber were futile, rolled onto his back, his eyes wide, his face resolute and his mouth closed in defiance.

"Poison? POISON? I'll gie ye *poison!* Maybe then *I'll* get some peace. Dae ye know how long Ah've been putting up with this? Whit Ah've suffered aw these years? Aw because o yer claptrap." She stood in front of the window hands on hips, her shadow spreading over him. He cowered in the bed like the mischievous child awaiting punishment from his mother.

"It's no claptrap," he squeaked, "it's a medical condition. There's even a word for whit Ah've got in the dictionary!"

"Ay, it's under 'L' for 'Lunacy'."

"Ay, very funny. Got oanymair? Ah could dae wi a laugh. It's no lunacy. Ah've told ye afore, it's called triskaidekaphobia." McGurk took great pride in being able to pronounce his condition, and even greater pride in being able to pronounce it without having to draw a breath.

"Triskak – triskep – triska-whit? Ye know Ah could never say thon word. Oanyway, Ah don't care if it's in the dictionary – gimme wan good reason for no likin the number 13."

"Wan good reason? Ah'll gie ye a brilliant wan – Maggie Thatcher wis born on the 13th o the month. Is that no good enough?"

"Ah, fair enough, Ah'll let ye awa wi that. But it's still nae reason for this rigmarole." Even she had to yield to his last point. That was *one* good reason. "Ah'm no taking oanymair o this. Ah'm goin doon tae the shops. Is there oanythin ye want me tae get for ye while Ah'm oot? Like arsenic? The phone number o a good psychiatrist? A full frontal lobotomy?"

"You fair crack me up hen. But since ye ask, ye can get a new fuse for that wee lamp o'er there. The auld wan's knackered – sort a like yersel!" A smug grin crawled up his face, his last put-down particularly satisfying.

"Jis you watch it pal, or Ah'll get ye they spiced buns ye're so fond o – a *baker's dozen* o them!" She now wore a radiant, false-teeth-baring grin, and merrily pranced out of the room. It was a few minutes past one o'clock that afternoon when she returned and found McGurk still in bed, but once again deep asleep. She took a few seconds to think to herself. Waking him once was merely an accident, waking him twice would be – fun!

She stalked toward the great iron bedstead, pursed her lips, and BLEW. The sound which issued forth from her was a glass-shattering, ear-drum piercing, ultra-sonic scream of a whistle, which had the potential to attract dogs from miles around. It also had the desired effect on her brother.

He moved swifter than he had done in years, sat bolt upright in bed, breathing heavily and staring with wild eyes at his sister. "Jeezo wumman! Whit are ye trying tae dae – kill me? Nae wonder Ah've got a bad heart."

"Bad heart? You never had a heart in the first place!" The pleasure of this exchange was evident on her face. She pulled the requested fuse from a pocket, and extracting a screwdriver from a drawer, moved to the "knackered" lamp and began to disassemble the plug. "Ah suppose Ah'll need tae dae this, unless ye've managed to get o'er this thirteen fixation . . ."

"Will ye stop saying that . . ."

"Whit? Thirteen?" she cut him off mid-sentence, agitating him further, her concentration more on winding him up than on the task she now embarked upon. She pulled out the old fuse, discarded it and tried to fumble the new one into the retaining clips.

"Haud yer wheesht will ye!"

"Ah will not 'Haud my wheesht', as ye put it. When will ye realise it's a load o mince? When ye're eighty? Ninety? When ye get yer telegram fae wee Lizzie in big Buck Hoose? When ye're deid?" She screwed the cover back onto the plug, and pressed it into the socket.

"Dae ye no realise that it's bad luck? An sayin it today jist makes it worse! It's like committing an act o blasphemy oan the day o the Sabbath! Ye'll be damned for it wumman, ye'll be damned for it."

"Ach, away an claw yer semmit! Ye're heid's fu o broken boatles. Bad luck my hin-end! I'll show ye it's no bad luck! 13, 13, 13, THIRTEEN, thirteen, thirteen, thirteen, thir-" Repeating the number, watching McGurk wince each time, she reached over to the switch on the lamp.

It was on the 13th minute of the 13th hour of the 13th day that she pushed the switch into the 'On' position. The current pulsated through the lamp, melting the already faulty wiring and two things hit McGurk's sister simultaneously. One was 240 volts, and the other the realisation that she had replaced the five amp fuse with one of the *thirteen* amp variety . . .

Reviews

Irish Fiction

Irish fiction writers have become renowned international novelists in the past decade. The narrative skills of Brian Moore, William Trevor and Edna O'Brien attract as many reviews as more eclectic scenarios coming from Roddy Doyle, Dermot Bolder and J F Donleavy. Mammy Ireland, having enjoyed but then dismissed and divorced the Dada, has sent the angst-informed Baby to Frankfurt. If only it was so simple. It may all have begun with Yeats's great valedictory poem: 'The Circus Animals' Desertion' is the first, post *Ulysses*, modern Irish novel. First line, chapter headings flesh out novelists and themes.

Verse/Chapter One: *I sought a theme and sought for it in vain.* Beckett, the diary-pillaging Aiden Higgins, the ever-questing Jennifer Johnston reply with versions on expectations and raise further doubts.

Chapter Two: *What can I but enumerate old themes? Godded and Codded* (1970) said Julia O'Faolain. *Victims* (1976) wrote Eugene McCabe. *Bogmail* (1978) reiterated Patrick McGinley and Dermot Healey whispered about *Banished Misfortune and Other Stories* (1982). As counterpoint Bernard MacLaverty released *Secrets and Other Stories* (1977).

Chapter Three: *And then a counter-truth filled out its play.* John Broderick's mis-shapen natives, impaled on spires, entombed in nunneries. The mirror-distorted fact-loaded fictions of Francis Stuart. The marvellous past-recreations of Seamus Deane, Kevin Casey, Ronan Sheehan and Ronan Bennett slip into our imaginative cognisance.

Chapter Four: *She, pity-crazed, had given her soul away.* Follow the stories of Maeve Binchy. Near behind her Dermot Bolger picks at the silver at the back of the same mirror. Tom Murphy (*The Seduction of Morality*, 1994), Michael P Harding (*The Trouble with Sarah Gullion*, 1988), Liam Lynch (*Tenebrae*, 1985) and Sean MacMathuna (*The Atheist*, 1988) have more in common with Deirdre Maddan than they might feel at ease with. Myopic visionaries also have time for dreams and may only talk in nightmares.

Chapter Five: *The Fool and Blind Man stole the bread.* Patrick McGinley, Patrick McCabe, Patrick Boyle, the gender-changed daughters of Lear pillage the bleak emotional heartlands of Patrick Kavanagh's Patrick Maguire in *The Great Hunger.* Touching the braille nerves ends are Maurice Leitch, Eoin McNamee, Meave Kelly, Nina Fitzpatrick, Clare Boylan and Bridget O'Connor.

Chapter Six: *Those masterful images became complete/ Grew in pure mind.* Back to Beckett. Stylish evocations of ageing by John McGahern. Urban ruins of mankind recalled in John Banville's excavations of the vain and the vulnerable. In American Colm McCann. In Cavan Dermot Healy.

Coda:. . . but out of what began?
A mound of refuse or the sweepings of a street,
Old kettles, old bottles, and a broken can,
Old iron, old bones, old rages, that raving slut
Who keeps the till. Now that my ladder's gone,
I must lie down where all the ladders start,
In the foul rag-and-bone shop of the heart.

This introduction, of course, also suggests a short story. The Irish riposte to the Irish joke:

Irish labourer meets British foreman on site:
Q. Paddy, do you know the difference between joist and girder? A. Sure, Joyce wrote *Ulysses* and Goethe *Faust.*

A significant figure in the promotion of the short story, and indeed much of the new writing represented in this issue is David Marcus. He precedes, overlaps and projects. Born into the Jewish community in Cork in 1924 he is married to the distinguished novelist Ita Daly. *Irish Writing* (1946-57) was his first editorial endeavour. Samuel Beckett, Mary Lavin and Brendan Behan made notable debutes. In 1967 his weekly 'New Irish Writing' page in *The Irish Press* became a showcase for emerging voices over the next two decades. John Banville, John McGahern and numerous others earned audiences in what the late John Jordan called "the needle-eye packed maelstrom of angelic tapestries". Marcus continues to encourage contracted fictions.

Irish Short Stories 1998 (Phoenix) captures

16 authors out on a creative wing. *The Makers* by Eilis Ni Dhuibhne is a fine drawn story of emotional entrapment. The most amazing new name/contribution is *The Outfielder. The Indian Giver* by Blanaid McKinney. On the surface it is a rite-of-passage for a sports writer, in unlikely tandem with a historian on the other side of America, baseball and Indians being their interests. Then emerges the tragic tale of the Choctow tribe, remembering their own 'Trail of Tears', subscribing to Irish Famine victims in the 1840s. A stadium that was an encampment is the scene of a dramatic *denouement*. Cultures elide. Explore.

Another discovery of Marcus (in 1992) is Colum McCann, now an award winning novelist based in New York. The writing is lucid and evocative. Compassionate insights into the dispossessed fuse his second novel *This Side of Brightness* (Phoenix £15.99). Set in the subways of New York, and the vertigo inducing heights strutted by steeplejacks, this is a marvellous evocation of extremes.

Extremes meet also in Sebastian Barry's novel *The Whereabouts of Eneas McNulty* (Picador). Betrayals, personal and political, mirror this writer's Dramatic preoccupations (see review of Irish Drama). Courage created by adversity is again central. Eneas, based in the boglands of Sligo, suffers the travails of his near namesake in Virgil. But there is a brutal rebuttal of sentimentality. "Arms and the man, I sing" says Virgil. Here the re-aligned Irish mythology of Pub-patriotism is not served. Innocence lost is replaced by a loss of identity. "Anger supplies the arms". These words are weapons, as Czech writer Jaroslav Seifert wrote: "We do not forgive in the name of love/ The sins of men/ We firmly avenge in the name of love/ The starving lives.

Creativity through love and fear is also a focus in Patrick McCabe's *Breakfast on Pluto* (Picador). Patrick Bryden, the central character, lives in Tyreelin in Co Monagahan on the partition-based border of Ireland. This is an imaginative re-siting of Inniskeen where Patrick Kavanagh's impotent Patrick Maguire railed against absentee sensualists in his long howl of a poem 'The Great Hunger' (1942).

Bryden is a transvestite, a prostitute 'abroad' in both Ireland and London and an illegitimate son of a priest 'at home'. Central to this brutal but paradoxically beautiful insight into a complex isolation is the evocation of the malevolent anti-Irish campaigns that precipitated major judicial aberrations in the 70s and 80s.

In a very odd way this 'led-madness' pervades Mark McCormack's first novel *Crowe's Requiem* (Cape). Set in the west of Ireland it has a Faustian figure emerge from a village called Furnace. Hell burns. He chooses his own name aged five . . . after a wind-battered creature falls from the skies at his earth-bound feet. Icarus meets Dedalus. Crowe adds the 'e' to "put some distance between himself and that fallen bird". The rest of his short life is imaginative misadventure. Light years away from British designated 'magical realism', this is realistic magic given literary flight.

An angel also appears in Jennifer Johnston's new novel *Two Moons* (Headline). Bonifacio di Longero captivates and releases the soul of elderly Mimi in the kingdom of Dalkey outside Dublin. Her actress daughter is Gertrude in *Hamlet*. Mischance creates mischief. As ever with Johnston the shift between reality and illusion is so slight that one must re-read to see the nuances from the nonsense. I envy readers coming to this beautifully-paced miniature for the first time. I expect my first paragraphs to attract criticism as 'agenda-imposed conclusions', like the quoted full stanzas of Yeats. A final piece of fictional association. John Banville's first publication was a seam set of scenarios called *Long Lankin* (1970). In the 'revised edition' of 1984 he subtracted the novella *The Possessed* and added as a final story 'De Rerum Natura', quarried from Lucretius. It opens

The old man was hosing the garden when the acrobats appeared. They were unexpected, to say the least. Elves, now would not have surprised him, or goblins. But acrobats!

The nature of Irish fiction is moving at the same pace as the politics. In our circus a new correctness has become the commonplace of invention. Out have gone the Animals. The Acrobats reign supreme.

Irish Poetry

Yeats framed the fictions. Now follows 18 statements of poetic facts around the versifying descendents of Joyce, a re-possession of the meandering *Ulysses*.

Seamus Heaney: *Opened Ground: Poems 1966-96* (Faber) is an updated *Selected* with the bonus of the text of his 1995 Nobel Lecture (see introduction). For the bibliophile the original full speech appears in *Crediting Poetry* (Gallery). The poems reveal in their entirety a rhythmic epitaph for an eroding past in a far from rural Ireland. The prose signposts an informed future.

Thomas Kinsella: *Collected Poems 1956-94* (OUP) is rewardingly read with *The Dual Tradition* (Carcanet), explained in the subtitle as 'An Essay on Poetry and Politics in Ireland'. The poems range from those in the mould-shattering *Downstream* (1962) to the Peppercanister sequences since 1972. The prose educates a perspective on Gaelic/English matters in a way that is not subservient to the academically superimposed 'Anglo-Irish Tradition'. Individual titles of the Peppercanister poems are published in beautiful limited editions from Dedalus.

Pearse Hutchinson is best encountered through *Selected Poems* and *The Soul that Kissed the Body* (both Gallery). The latter contains poems in Irish with translations into English and lyrical introduction by the author. As befits a fine translator of Spanish poets, Lorca is a shadow evoked on reading Hutchinson. Lorca spoke of *Pena* "not anguish because with *Pena* one can smile". He also wrote of *Duende* "the hidden spirit of disconsolate pain". These intensities inform all of Hutchinson's best work. I also recommend the cassette *Danta/Poems* (Clo Iar-Chonnachta).

Always on the edge of edge of Europe, metaphorically and often physically, are the creatures that inhabit Michael Longley's *Selected Poems* (Cape) and the beautifully produced small edition *Broken Dishes* (Abbey). War memories are shared verbal shrapnel. Battle wounded are the animals in his beastiary. A more melancholic compassion infuses recent titles from his contemporary Derek Mahon:

The Hudson Letter and *The Yellow Book* (both Gallery). If the former evokes exile in America, it is as an emotional emigre, "a rueful veteran of the gender wars" Mahon touches his subject matter with braille tenderness, in the second. As can be seen from his new poems in this issue Patrick Galvin knows how to record the moments when extremes meet. His *New and Selected Poems* (Cork University Press) is essential reading for all interested in Irish Furies and tale-bearing fairies.

> Hearts with one purpose alone
> Through summer and winter seem
> Enchanted to a stone
> To trouble a living stream
> – Yeats, 'Easter 1916'

It is regrettable that all too often poet-publishers find their own work marginalised or ignored. This must not happen to Peter Fallon, John F Deane and Adrian Rice. Fallon: *News of the World: Selected and New Poems* (Gallery) brings an urban eye to rural sophistications. The poems are universal in theme but curiously and pleasingly private in declaration. Deane's *The Stylized City: New and Selected Poems* (Dedalus) is marvellously supplemented by the recent *Christ, with Urban Fox* (both Dedalus) which also carries a startling cover by John Behan. Here wisdom lies in the observations. Never judgemental. Sharp but never cruel. Evocative of "imaginary possessions". Newest, to me, Adrian Rice: *Impediments* (Abbey). His "God is shifting the furniture", "what's happening in happening inside". A lively dance of a debut.

An important part of the Dedalus intent is to bring translations of continental writers to the islanders. Here comes a mid-flow catechism. *At the Year's Turning*, edited by Marco Sonzogni draws on over 100 Irish poets 'responding' to the work of the great Italian writer Giocomo Leopardi (1798-1837). Among those familiar to *Chapman* readers Heaney, Kinsella, Eithne Strong and Jean O'Brien. Deane himself translated from the French Anise Koltz: *At the Devil's Banquets*. Most recent titles from Italian and French respectively are Edoardo Sanguineti: *Libretto* translated by Padraig J Daly and Jean Orizet: *Man and his Masks*; translated by Pat Boran. Finally a special ripple of applause for Desmond O'Grady's *Ten Modern Arab Poets*. This is as good a way as any to confer with this most cosmopolitan of Irish commentators.

Dublin loves informed bombast. Brendan Kennelly is Kerry's gift to the city. He is prolific in literary and personal terms. I, like many, embrace his friendship as armour against indifference. Though I must admit I did escape untouched by ethics when he was my 'Moral Tutor' in Trinity College, Dublin in the 60s. Emotionally he has felt death, adored love and condemned any complicity with pomp while exuding self-pride and confidence. He has published over 30 titles, many including poems, all diverse and entertainingly poetic. *Poetry My Arse* is a series of shouts against complacency. *The Man Made of Rain* (both Bloodaxe) is a serene, redeeming, contemplative reflection after a near-death experience on a surgeon's table. Minute but beautiful, at the tail end of 1998, comes *The Singing Tree* (Abbey). To accompany it the Newry company have also published two intriguing chapbooks Joan Newmann's *Thin Ice* and Catherine Graham's *The Watch*.

Central to any overview must be solid trees in the forest. Robert Greacen is one of these vital figures who give root nurture to a nation's literature. I particularly recommend for an understanding of political fusions his autobiography *The Sash My Father Wore* (1997). His most recent poetry collection is *Protestant Without a Horse* (Laggan). To be read in conjunction with Gorgonzola and burgundy and Padraic Fiacc's *Red Earth* followed by Hugh Maxton's *Wakening: An Irish Protestant Upbringing*, both from Laggan.

Of the dark past
A child is born;
With joy and grief
My heart is torn.
– Joyce, 'Ecce Puer'

On the outskirts of Dublin, sea-sided, lives Eithne Strong, a stick of dynamite camouflaged by wool. She has, first with her husband Rupert and Runa Press, more recently with a number of 'feminist led' publishers,

articulated the individual vision of the poet as opposed to the separate nature of the polemicist. She has been an advocate for debunking masculine vanities without losing touch with the comradeship of loyalties. Her long, brutal but meditative poem *Flesh – The Greatest Sin* (1980) is New Ireland's reply to the fearful impotency that informed Kavanagh's *The Great Hunger* (1942). It is not in *Spatial Nosing: New and Selected Poems* (Salmon). But therein lies a unique record of the "dark hard tie(s)" of love and the "breaking labour" that leads to subsequent regeneration in motherhood. Strong has influenced many new writers, not always to good effect, but one whom she inspires with empathy's strength is Galway based Eva Bourke. *Spring in Henry Street* (Dedalus) breathes of a European curiosity rather than insular introspection. German born she first of all explores the past and then allows the poems to excavate her discoveries. In a curiously resonant way the writer most bearing echoes of Strong is a man. Francis Devine's *Red Star, Blue Moon* (Elo Publications) rushes to record the moment. As Pearse Hutchinson says in his forward sometimes the result is "prosaic" but the energy is welcome and this is a good introduction to a new voice.

Obvious craft and dedication sometimes obscures the vulnerable, bruised nature of poets. Two moments to stop and stare. Dublin based, widely travelled, consumed by the urge to write – and always write well – Macdara Woods: *Selected Poems* (Dedalus) encompasses a life articulate. Head of Humanities in Waterford Regional Technical College, John Ennis is the discovery of the past decade. "Rich and allusive" (John Jordan). His *Selected Poems* (Dedalus) are essential for a broader understanding of the new questioning of imperatives that is rescuing Ireland from old pieties.

Beautiful land the patriot said
and rinsed it with his blood. And the sun rose.
And the river burned. The earth leaned
towards him: Shadows grew long. Ran red.
Beautiful land I whispered. But the roads
stayed put. Stars froze in the suburb.
Shadows iced up. Nothing moved.
Except my hand across the page. And these

words. (– Eavan Boland, 'Whose?')

One wanders about in an afternoon of reading. Down in Kerry the energetic Gabriel Fitzmaurice has in Gaelic, with an introduction by Alan Titley, new poems *Giolla na nAmhran* (Coisceim). In English *The Village Sings* (Peterloo) and then, wearing his anthologist's cap, the highly recommended *Poems I Wish I'd Written* (Clo Iar-Chonnachtan). This is selected translations by Fitzmaurice of Irish poets as diverse as Anon and the wonderful, much missed Caitlin Maude. Up the coast in Limerick dwells Ciaran O'Driscoll. His fourth collection is *The Old Woman of Magione* (Dedalus). Here are religious depths, visions and beliefs enunciated without secretarian shallows, illuminating of a most original thinker, challenging from a most expressive of writers. Further up the Atlantic coast, in Galway, one finds Fred Johnston, annotator of John Behan's art, fiction writer and poet. *True North* (Salmon) demonstrates the lucid direction of this engaging and engaged of minds. Cutting across the midlands where Gallery Press and the hard to contact Desmond Egan reside one returns to literary Dublin. In Parnell Square, in the Writers' Centre, Peter Sirr collates, assembles, shakes and regenerates attitudes and opinions (he is Director). *The Ledger of Fruitful Exchange* (Gallery) moves us through his Fair. Out in the suburbs, reflecting new confidences are Patrick Deeley: *Turane: The Hidden Village* and Paddy Bushe: *Digging Towards the Light* (both Dedalus).

Flight into Reality is the title of Rosemarie Rowley's cassette version of her 1989 text (Rowan Tree Press). Landings in imagination mark Aiden Matthews; *According to the Small Hours* (Cape) and two latest books from the admirable Michael O'Siadhail *A Fragile City* and *Our Double Time* (both Bloodaxe). Into this kaleidoscope of the new, time should also be made for Mark Roper: *Catching the Light* (Laggan) and *The Home Fire* (Abbey).

"... here I am, up to my usual tricks,/ evoking spring-time on the least pretext,– Derek Mahon, 'Landscape after Baudelaire'". "I love a poem that sends critical skin and hair flying"– Biddy Jenkinson, speaking at the Writers Centre, May 1998.

Penelope penultimate. One of the great titles of 1993 was Enda Wyley; *Eating Baby Jesus* (Dedalus). It was marketed for Christmas. Ms Wyley proves she is more than a title-maker with *Socrates in the Garden* (Dedalus). She is now Poet in Residence at Melbourne University and the poems give flesh to ghosts and voices to Bees. She is a marvel. The great Scottish writer Fred Urquhart spent a Bloomsday afternoon with myself and Trevor Royle early in the 90s in his flat overlooking the hurdles of Musselburgh Race Course. Out of a very blue story he suddenly announced "Leland Bardwell, best-named of poets, she knows how to do it". He was right. Her *The White Beach: New and Selected Poems 1960-98* (Salmon) proves it.

"I have been infinitely caused" she says and then builds up poems that are untidy, lived-in, comfortable dwellings ... if you avoid the dry rot and stay out of the draughts. Other mansions are occupied by Eavan Boland. Her *Collected Poems* (1995) and the beautifully written meditation on an autobiography *Object Lessons* (1996) inform the voice of experience overheard in *The Lost Land* (Carcanet). Culture and creativity are her themes. Wounded ghosts are her protagonists. The result is a book with the power of pleasure. Shock is the initial response to Aine Ni Ghlinn: *Deoradh Nar Caoineadh/Unshed Tears* (Dedalus). Translated by Padraig O Snodaigh this is a sequence of tough poems about abuse. Child-abuse, self-abuse, abuse at abasement, affront at apathy. This is the strongest evidence yet that complicity by silence about such matters is a thing of the past. Yes.

Coda: of course I cheat. Behind the Hill of Howth lies a horizon. As dreams regain the day reality intervenes. An admired but missing name among contributors and those reviewed is Paul Durcan. Harvill and Hayden now announce his new collection will appear in February 1999. *The Mary Robinson Years: 100 Poems*. Inspiration walks. So do all my Irish Familiars

Irish Drama

Brian Friel's *Philadelphia, Here I Come!* (1964) featured a split-stage and a dual central character. 'Public' Gareth was "the one people see, talk to, talk about". 'Private' Gar is an "unseen man, the man within, the conscience". Following its Dublin premiere the Stage-Irish Stereotype exited, stage-right, pursued by sentimentality. Obsolete. Entering from the left came the strutting Irish Staged Paradox, prompted by a new generation of actors and critics.

Duality preoccupied dramatist and audiences; political partition, bilingualism, rural/urban divides. In 'character' the dual-tradition of Anglo-Irish literature was topical, relevant, dramatic and on-stage. This emphasis shift, stretching over a generation, is epitomised in the plays of Sebastian Barry and Tom Murphy. A substantial selection of their works are collected in attractive and comparatively cheap editions in the series of *Methuen Contemporary Dramatists* (all £9.99).

Sebastian Barry, Writer in Residence at the Abbey Theatre, was born in 1955 in Dublin to poet/architect Francis Barry and actress Joan O'Hara ("the most eloquent legs in Europe": Harold Hobson, *The Sunday Times*). Initially he published poetry but since 1986 he has primarily been seen as a dramatist. He has had seven plays staged. In 1996 he was awarded the £10,000 Ireland Funds Literary Prize. Five of his plays are collected in one volume with an incisive introduction by Fintan O'Toole. The 1995 successes in Dublin, London and New York of the short *The Only True History of Lizzie Finn* (90 mins) and the sublime *The Steward of Christendom* are given contextual depth when read with *Prayers of Sherkin*.

Lizzie, at the turn of the century, moves from Music Hall to Big House to expose a dissembling establishment. Quaker Fanny Hawke, a real-life ancestor of the dramatist, abandons the isle of Sherkin to marry the Catholic lithographer Patrick Kirwin in the mainland town of Baltimore. Thomas Dunne, a former British policeman in Dublin, the 'Stewart' of the title, finds little Christianity as an indigent in a County Home run by Republican sympathisers. In all three plays there is a remapping of regional memory, an exorcism of traditional pieties and the deliverance of a dissenting secular voice. This is not revisionism, rather a renewal of debate.

In the mid 30s James Joyce wrote to his friend Frank Budgen "I have a grocer's assistant's mind". Thomas Murphy was born in 1935 in Tuam, Co Galway , in the west of Ireland. His early play *A Whistle in the Dark* (1961) was rejected by the Abbey but became a critical and commercial success in London. A false start. He returned to Ireland and The National Theatre, under new management, produced a series of his plays that examine and unravel the vulnerable Irish male in a society governed by the Catholic church and ruled by devout mothers. The major works are *A Crucial Week in the Life of a Grocer's Assistant* (1969), *The Morning after Optimism* (1971), *The Sanctuary Lamp* (1976), *The Blue Macushla* (1980) and *The Gigli Concert* (1981).

In 1985 he returned to Galway as Writer in Residence for The Druid Theatre Company, Fringe First Award winners in the early 80s. There he produced *Conversations on a Homecoming* and *Bailegangaire*. The latter evoking a soul-searching performance as the manipulative Mommo by the late Siobhan McKenna. In 1991 *The Patriot Game* was produced in The Tramway, Glasgow.

Murphy's plays fill four volumes in the Methuen series. Again Fintan O'Toole introduces them: he has for those interested written a marvellous study of Murphy *The Politics of Magic* (Raven Arts Press: 1987 £5.95). He divides the plays thematically rather than chronologically. Again a new dimension is given to the reader. Historical perspectives are challenged. The rhetoric of James in *Optimism* finds plaintive echo in the whinge of Francisco in *Sanctuary*. Internal exiles are exposed, sexually and politically in *Gigli* and *Conversations*. The overall impression is of language releasing confusions. Articulated anarchy emerging from domestic silence. It is a unique and uncomfortable world and as such important theatrically.

"It wasn't an awareness of direction being changed but of experience being of a totally different order." (Brian Friel: *Translations*)

Edinburgh Book Festival

The Irish Times report on the 1997 Edinburgh Book Festival opened "Shambles were singing in Charlotte Square". What a difference a year makes. This year's Festival, under a new administrator (Faith Liddell), in its first year as an annual event, has been *the* success story of the many festivities in Edinburgh's August culture bash.

Intelligent programming is the basic reason for this. Mornings (10.15am) over the seventeen days started with a writer, or several writers on a theme, meeting in packed audiences over coffee and croissants in the Spiegeltent. Quality varied from interesting to fantastic. There was, however, an unintentional distraction. Ms Diana Hope, the regular chair, became an unwitting focus of attention. Her use, often deserved, of the epithet 'Superb' became a mantra. Bets were taken. Fourteen, on the morning with A L Kennedy, won. Ms Hope's wide-eyed questioning of the same writer, "You do use words, don't you?", got the most eloquently raised Dundee eyebrow of the Festival.

Late mornings allowed a variety of 'Meet the Author' sessions (11.30am). Opening day saw Baroness James cut the tapes and then dash into a tent to give a brisk, entertaining session as P D James, the writer. Jeanette Winterson, sharply avoiding verbal sniping from a Scots based literary agent, was lucid and audience-friendly. As was Iain Banks. Bruce Robinson, alcoholically challenged, was not. He lost everything but the bottle before re-staggering later in the afternoon. Nick Hornby was a charmer, never mind the hype this is a writer, an observer, a nice man. Louis de Bernier was not, this time. Ian Rankin, as ever, was fun. Readers of *Chapman* may pretend not to know of him. His ten novels in paperback unravel the lifetime umbrages of Inspector Rebus. Rebus, on a good day, finds solace – like many – in *The Oxford Bar*. Bad days he returns there for another kind of solution. The pathologist in his novels began life as the cadaverous Professor Gates. The new short story he read to a packed tent this August had one transfixed listener as Rankin elaborated on the growth and girth of the Professor. This was John Gates, Manager of 'The Ox'. "He grows into the part," said his wife Margaret later. She may have been plaintive. "Malicious . . . but accurate" was the general judgement among the corpulent males who rolled up, wearing pub ties (bovine above a grille) for a 'Night of Scottish Crime' which turned into a catwalk of Rankin, Manda Scott, Val McDermid, Christopher Brookmyre and an anodyne Paul Johnston. A convocation of red herrings.

The James Thin sponsored 'Lunchtime Readings' meant writers as diverse as poets George Szirtes and Fleur Adcock, novelists Douglas Kennedy and Josie Lloyd and biographer Ferdinant Mount were listened to through munched rolls and slurped soft drinks. The abbreviated performance by Dublin writer Lana Citron and fellow fiction writers Geoff Ryman and Jenny McLeod showed scant respect for the audience, no matter how small. The highlight for me, in this slot, was Donny O'Rourke with Helen Dunmore. Choral psalms of sensitivity from both poets. Dunmore notates the sacred. O'Rourke was revelational in how he caught the tone of the day . . . post Omagh . . . and literally sang of love familial, and, in the finest way, patriotic.

Waterstones stepped bravely in to sponsor the afternoon slot 'The Bigger Picture' (3.30pm). Audiences were small but this quickly became the focal point of my day. Israeli David Grossman, a novelist by art, a polemicist by conviction spoke of the conscience having imperative power over political expediency. His brave commentary on governmental treatment of his Palestinian neighbours *The Yellow Wind* (1988) was culturally paralleled by his novel of lost innocence *The Zig-Zag Kid* (1998). He is with Yehda Amichai (1995) and Amos Oz (1997) another ambassador for human faith, informing the mind with understanding rather than religious dogma. London's Israeli Embassy is to be congratulated on sending such cultural dissidents to this devolving nation.

Others who lifted the mind in this slot were Luc Sante (Belgium), Adeline Yen Mah (China), Shani Mootoo (Canada), Vikram Chandra (India), Simon Louvish (Scotland) and in a session fired with further fury at the obscene murder and mayhem in Omagh truly a great reading by the Irish novelists Jennifer Johnston and Bernard MacLaverty. Another searing and rewarding hour came with the appearance of the great Portuguese writer Mario de Carvalho. In a session, chaired knowledgably and sympathetically by Christopher Whyte, de Carvalho read from his allegorical novel *A God Strolling in the Cool of the Evening*. Iberian pain at Roman dictates gave focus to the surface narrative, subjection, mental and political, underpinned the insight of this man. A lawyer, exiled by Salazar, he returned to his native country an acclaimed novelist a decade ago. Only three Scots were in the audience of 12.

Many Scots attended Irvine Welsh, even more turned out for Kenneth White. The asinine assumption: "You're either a White person or you're not" has stifled, in an obsessive way, any objective response to the work of this intelligent, charming man. But in no way can he be claimed "the greatest Scottish thinker since MacDiarmid".

The quiet humanism of Robin Jenkins reinforced this opinion. The subversive avoidance of categories by William MacIlvanney reinforced my judgement. Creativity, original, and not allied to vague ecology or escapist environmentalism; should be examined more closely. These views became confirmation as on separate mornings Edwin Morgan and Alan Spence showed that assimilation of world cultures is rewarded by pragmatic Scottish enlightenment.

Further post-colonial generosity was evident from Edinburgh's American Consulate, celebrating its bicentenary by bringing together such gender opposites, but soul-mates, as novelists Edmund White and Joyce Carol Oates. He was liberated libido. She was angst articulate. The other great American spirit appeared on the final day in a calm reading, haiku-infused by the presence as Scottish guest of Spence and Kevin MacNeil. Lucian Stryk superimposed tender compassion over unsentimental observations. His Japanese/Chinese translations should need no introduction to a poetry reading audience. But, shamefully, his rare and rewarding appearance was unrecorded by Scottish press or media.

There were, of course, moments of epiphany. Gitta Sereney, with Magnus Linklater as an exemplary Chair, became informatively defensive about complicity through cupidity with criminals. Seventy year old novelist Alan Sillitoe, nervously pecking out a greeting on his morse code black box, allowed nerve-tugging insight into despair. A diluted aftermath to a lunchtime dilemma made Giles Gordon unintentionally slur of the year. Joan Lingard, Brian Patten and Roger McGough, in very different ways, but with common respect for empathy, earned a new generation of readers. This eliding of age-groups, the creation of future audiences, is the great, lasting virtue of Ms Liddells's first directorship.

Her staff were young, eager and knowledgable, a delight for this tired old hack to admire and collaborate with. As for the last three Book Festivals, I enrolled my neighbour's daughters Megan and Emma to enable us to cover over 90 events for *The Irish Times* (and now *Chapman*). This year, unlike last year, we came out of the tented gardens metaphorically singing "Sweet Dreams and Dancing are in Charlotte Square".

Edinburgh International Festival and Fringe 1998

First of all my thanks to the Editor of *Chapman* for this opportunity to document Festival 1998. I was this year, as I have been since returning to Edinburgh in 1992, the accredited reviewer/critic for Dublin's *The Sunday Tribune*. I will elaborate later. Suffice to say that this August real life and death meant art was sidelined. Few Edinburgh notices appeared in Ireland after Omagh.

My international Festival opened on Sunday 16 August with Berlioz's *Grande Messe des Morts* (Usher Hall). Conductor Donald Runnicles, the Edinburgh Festival Chorus and Gregory Turay (tenor) sang "I groan like a guilty man/ Oh God, spare a prayer". The casualties of nationalist imperatives, the obscene details of the murder and mayhem in Ireland were filtering in. Statistics have no soul, so no numbering here of the dead. Only time for a prayer.

By the time this human-shattering event occurred I had already covered ten days of the Fringe. There were moments of enlightenment, delight, charm and one of appalling insensitivity compounded by crass arrogance.

Arnold Wesker's *Letter to a Daughter* (Assembly Rooms) featured Julie Clare as composer/chantress hearing wisdom's hymn. It was choral dualism between consenting artists. Wesker's text and lyrics, married to the music of Ben Till, gave birth (unlikely image, I know!) to a magnificent performance by Clare. Behind her, through a transparent screen, six musicians teased the air harmoniously to complement her. It was magic.

Across the city Theatre Talipot from Renuin Island, Mauritius, performed *The Water Carriers*. Home is the Indian Ocean. The rhythms of water, wave and tidal variants were both echoes and Furies. The climate punctuated the choreography. St Bride's glowed.

With fourteen performances the Traverse Theatre deservedly was focus for local and visiting press-attention. Sometimes this led to an exclusive concentration of compliant heads. Hilary Strong's decision to shift Fringe timetable away from International Festival schedule meant I attended all the Traverse openings before 16 August.

A brief comment. Ms Strong has in her five years as Director made the Fringe a more democratic, audience friendly, part of the overall assembly of Festivals in Edinburgh. Yet it may be the largest element in the overall cultural structure but it is intrinsically important *only* by association with the other events.

To autocratically declare autonomy is to fail to appreciate the aspirations of locals to be seen by visitors and the ambition of visitors to be judged in relation to the International artists invited by Brian McMaster. She is weakening the whole by pandering to a false sense of individuality. In plain terms, 'stubborn' is being camouflaged as 'common sense'.

Back to entertainment. At the Traverse, Sarah Kane's *Crave* allowed the intellect to engage with demanding contractions. Four talking figures; drawn from the visual world of Francis Bacon, manoeuvre under spotlights. Distortion lies in the longing to disturb. In 43 minutes fragmented lives interlock. Performers Sharon Duncan-Brewster, Ingrid Craigie, Paul Thomas Hickey and Alan Williams are mesmerising. Minimal movement allows nuance to become emphasis. Compulsively theatrical, dramatically memorable.

For several years Grassmarket Project (Director, Jeremy Weller) have brought emotional destitutes literally off the streets to mirror their existence for a theatre-going audience. It is a manipulative exercise I have always deplored. For the record I *have* seen all of Weller's productions and reviewed two of them. Refused to endorse any of the Fringe First Awards given to them by *The Scotsman*. This year was a shameful nadir. Complicity with warp given respectability of woof by the awarding of yet another Fringe First.

Soldiers emanated from a documentary-maker, and a medley of Squaddies, ex-squaddies and others demanding our time and attention for their obsessions. By Weller's intent they also were making claim for our respect. It was presented as theatre, an entertainment. It was a circus, Roman and carnal. An exploitation of egos on stage and in the audience. Nothing more than militarism rampant. "A crude use of this venue to propagate and sanitise brutality" I filed to Dublin.

That was dealing with it in theatrical terms. More important issues occupied my mind. After opening night it was obvious that 'Nick' on stage was Nic Glasnovic, a member of the Croatian HVO. A group, not to dignify them as a 'regiment', guilty of some of the most appalling atrocities in recent events in the Balkans. He paraded prejudice on stage. Some sniggered. There was applause at the end. I protested afterwards. I regret that professional curiosity made me complicitous with the performance on the night. I did not walk out. I waited for outrage. There was none. *Soldiers* was reviewed and awarded a *Scotsman* Fringe First. Then on the BBC 2's *Edinburgh Night's* Ken Lukowick, a soldier who had served in Bosnia, denounced Glasnovic face to face. Glasnovic left Scotland the next day. *Soldiers* closed. Jeremy Weller and the Traverse admitted to a serious error.

In *The Scotsman* (August 28), a fortnight after opening night, the previously reticent Joyce McMillan wrote that she "knew" when she "saw this big, twitchy, hyper-masculine figure walk on stage" with "his strange way of talking about women (babes)" she knew what he was. She did not write murderer or war-criminal. Her response was "slight shock" that this did not change her favourable, passive uninformative attitude to the initial performance.

Joyce McMillan is a critic and a social commentator who has a deservedly high reputation for truth-seeking and astuteness. She can also be assertive and adamant in declaring her convictions. Here she chose to be passive. In this she is paradoxically arrogant and insensitive to the ephemeral role entertainment and its reporters, and audiences for same, have in the real world.

My lines on *Soldiers* never saw print. People of the same sick mentality as Glasnovic saw to that. The dead and maimed deserve respect. Part of that must be to condemn their murderers . . . wherever. To applaud liberal attitudes at the expense of such imperatives is to lose sight of humanity and its demands on mind, heart and critical responses.

Rant over. A far more endearing representation of power decadent was Scarlet Theatre's *Princess Sharon* (Director, Katarzyna) also in the Traverse. Beautifully drilled the cast of twelve moved in homage to the great Kantor in this adaptation by Andrzej Sadowski of Witold Gombrowicz's *Princess*

Ivona. Inlaid in the performance was a devout satire on the commercial canonisation of a once powerful Princess of some land or another. An icon felled. Who dares to speak of Windsor or Wales in this context? In the title role there was a hauntingly beautiful performance by Sue Maund.

The two main Scottish productions of Liz Lochhead's *Perfect Days* and David Harrower's *Kill the Old Torture Their Young* will be familiar to readers of *Chapman*. Both were awarded Fringe Firsts.

Across from the Traverse, beyond the Meadows, in Southside, C Byrnes brought her third original play *Slags* from Newcastle to Edinburgh. It had a very late-night slot. *The Scotsman* reviewer (present on the same night as this commentator) coffined it in the self designated, and self-demeaning, 'Page of Shame' slot. He was wrong. It rippled with awareness that females may be complicitous with sleaze but emotionally they can equally be free of guilt. Bravely rhymed and plotted rhythmically it explored exploitation, and perceptions of same, in dramatic fashion.

Now to matters great and trivial at the International Festival. John Clifford's translation/adaptation of Calderón's *Life is a Dream* (1635) tenanted my mind for many months. It was directed in taut, abrupt scenes by the Catalan Calixto Bieito, interpreted by a multinational Lyceum Theatre Company in their home venue. In but two hours it devolved personal independence to an autonomous state governed by humane imperatives.

The theme is of pricked vanities. Heir apparent Segismundo (George Anton) is imprisoned by his insecure father, the King. Freed he turns into a liberated anarchist. Then he crosses the path of Rosura (Olwyen Fouere) who has been deserted by the ambitious Prince Astolfo (Nicholas Bailey). On a dim-lit set, atmospherically catching the black-sanded plains of Poland, tyranny succumbs to humanity. Anton's performance aches with his character's vanity, and consequent desperation. When, in an eye/mind-opening theatrical moment, he and Rosura embrace stoicism; in cruciform fashion; emotional deliverance rather that religious salvation defuses both angst and sentimentality.

In the same week came a full five act performance of *Don Carlos* (Festival Theatre). Five hours of near greatness from Verdi. And a distracting horse. Would Princess Liz (Karita Matilda) fall off? Would the horse leave a trademark? Would the dancers mount him? All passed, in a manner of speaking, decorously. Director Luc Bondy moved a huge cast across 16th century France/Spain as promenading palimpsets. Peace may come if French Elizabeth marries to the Spanish throne. But to whom, Carlos (Julian Gavin) or his father Philippe (Ferruccio Furlanetto)? Intrigue, mined by the Inquisition, provided, paradoxically, scenes of despair and torch-lit horror with performances of lyric depth and dramatic enlightenment. Conducted by Bernard Haitink; in what has proved to be his last touring appearance; this was a glorious return to Edinburgh by the financially troubled and personnel-divided Royal Opera (Covent Garden), Chorus and Orchestra.

As ever, since Brian McMaster took over as Director seven Festivals ago, I spread my Dance programme over all three weeks, the equivalent of leaving the sweetmeats at the edge of the plate. First came Pacific Northwest Ballet allowing us to see Balanchine's 1962 version of *A Midsummer's Night Dream* (Playhouse). I envied the children drawn from Edinburgh primary schools who became ankle nipping butterflies and fairies to an impish Puck (Seth Belliston) and the ever-so-near-embracing Titania (Anne Derleux) and Oberon (Paul Gibson). Summoning up beauty was an ethereal Butterfly (Kaoiri Nakamura). Part Two, in Theseus's Court, consisted of a *Divertissement* of rare beauty from Patricia Barker and Jeffrey Stanton. Performances like this could give kitsch a good name.

Earlier, in the same venue, was Companyia de Danse Gelabert-Azzorpardi's *ZumZum Ka*. It was mystifying, often visually disturbing, even threatening. The title, onomatopoeic Catalan for bees mustering their sting forces, conflicts with the oddness of 'K' in the once proscribed national tongue. Exorcism or assimilation? Kafka as stigmatic tourist in Sitges? As likely as any other interpretation. Reality fading back into shadowland is as good a prose translation as I can summon up.

By this stage the Festival was half-started. Finished it had presented one of the greatest ever Dance programmes.

Hans van Manen is *the* great 20th century European choreographer. From 1951 he had worked with the Dutch National Ballet. In 1960 he founded the breakaway Nederlands Dans Theatre. Brian McMaster, in a move deserving Nobel Peace Prize status, brought both companies to Edinburgh to pay tribute, dance attention to van Manen. Nederlands II & III were predictable (Playhouse). They were great. Passion came in two separate appearances from Dutch National. The loose and linear *Five Tangos* was loud and I loved it. Others said "trivial". *Three Pieces for Het* linked Willy Hines and Michael Flatley, though they would be "chilled" by comparison. I was told "old hat": serious dance critics do not hear a pun. Then came *Twilight* John Cage's enjambed minimal sound against a nuclear reactor background. Movement surged as protest. This was free-falling magic.

The finale will become Festival legend. *Live* had two dancers, Sabine Chaland and Gael Lambiotte. A camera catches them on stage, projecting facial close-ups on to an immense back-screen. Then they literally took to the aisles, the foyer, and the traffic-active High Street outside the theatre. Only the camera followed. The stage was abandoned. The City met Festival. Only a standing ovation brought them back indoors to the footlight's glow. Pleasure reigned.

Other lights tortured the retina during the mysterious, sometimes baffling, Peter Stein production of a new play by Botho Strauss *Die Ähnlichen* (Lookalikes). Inside a neon lit room three women groom themselves. Not MacBeth's witches, more Genet's Maids. In a series of loosely connected 'moral interludes' fate traps them in soul-reflecting dilemmas. Prostitution vies with child-abuse to manipulate our attention. Moving across the episodic biographies is a permanent figure, though a diverse persona. This is played by the great Dörte Lyssewski. One moment the 'paraperson' Magda, next the vamp Odile. Abruptly we have reached an Epilogue. We are back in the neon lit room. Four hours have passed. Time for grooming resumes.

Also in the Kings Theatre was the anarchic Carles Santos's *La Pantera Imperial*; 'A Homage to J S Bach'. Fugues and Preludes set off the actors into frenzied activity on a stage framed by a forest of stern-faced busts of the composer. Performers and busts swing. Buggery in a bird-bath was one of the quieter moments. Rarely in the history of this theatre have so many clothes fallen to the floor. According to the programme there were a mere seven performers. At any given moment, over this hour and a half light-fantastic, I was seeing hundreds.

The rich and varied music programme 'The Celebration of the Harp' has already been eloquently praised by Joy Hendry. I concur. I was gifted to hear Richard Goode play Mozart and watch Frans Brüggan conduct *The Orchestra of the 18th Century* (they play on the original instruments) in a series of pieces by Mendelssohn. He is not really 'my man', but the performance of his *Italian*, quick and light as migrating kingfishers, had me stomping away with the rest of an entranced audience.

This latter performance also provided a personal epiphany. The Press usually sit together. Sometimes even speak with each other. My neighbour was scribbling. I felt curious empathy. "Hayden Murphy, *Sunday Tribune*, Dublin" I said. He paled. He stared. In accented English he whispered "you published me, from Poland, thirty years ago". True in 1968, the year of International protests, I did publish Boleslaw Taborski, dissident. Now he is internationally renowned poet, playwright and translator of the Pope. We had only once met at a rally in the early 70s. Extinguishing grey hairs met and embraced as the years rolled back.

Brian McMaster has become the great planner of the Final week. A fact Hilary Strong should note if she again removes

Fringe box-office facilities. Once the Fireworks were the highlight. Now they have become a public display surrounded by private pleasures. Of course, there are exceptions. *Caligula* (Playhouse) was given an angst-loaded modern dress treatment, in Dutch translation, by Director Ivo van Hove. It would have benefited by the presence of the horse in *Don Carlos* in week one.

Van Hove, however, had earned respect the previous evening with his powerfully imagined presentation of Eugene O'Neill's *More Stately Mansions*. Ranging over four hours, featuring ten minutes of ballectic, highly charged, and yes erotic, nudity, what transfixed in the mind was the passion and fury in the writing. Possessive mother Deborah Harford (Joan MacIntosh), her son Simon (Tim Hopper) and her daughter-in-law Sara (Jenny Bacon) are impacted volcanoes. They rage against an impotent heat within. They are linked by earthly insecurity while hoping for redemption by fire. This play is literally unfinished business. O'Neill wanted the text burnt on his death. In this production it is given a dramatic afterlife. A peacock rather than a Phoenix arising from the flames.

Then came Luc Bondy's *Phèdre* (Kings Theatre). This was uninterrupted pleasure. Delivered in French, Racine's rancid questioning of the abuse of power was given a shot of dramatic violence. Destructive vanities dissembled before our eyes as Phèdre (Valérie Dréville) savagely castrates the lives of Thésée (Didier Sandre) and his son Hipplyte (Sylvain Jacques). Choreographed prose, lit by French poetics, emerged, unravelled over two hours.

The great pleasure of having the *Tribune* space has been my ability to target Festival's final night on a personal basis. My choice this year was Scottish Opera's *Dalibor* (Festival Theatre) which I'm delighted to see has entered the repertoire with a late appearance in Glasgow. Smetana's hymn for Czech independence (Director, David Pountney) was light opera given lyric treatment. Leo Marian Vodicken, in the title role, on a see-saw set, even managed to make the absurd finale convincing. Not credible but pleasurable. They all die in a surfeit of song. A delight.

Conscious that this commentary complements an Irish issue of *Chapman* a final word of praise for integration. *All Strange Away* is adapted from a 1973 prose piece by Beckett. Asylum Theatre (Director, Nigel Roper) evoke a marvellous solo performance from Mark Stuart Currie. In a sand pit of his own making the character is a human time-clock perpetually draining away. What is being present is not pessimism. It is humane salvation redeemed by ego. Theatre beyond frills.

Hayden Murphy

Other Books/Publications Received for Irish Issue

Arts:

Art in Ulster 1: 1557-1957: John Hewitt; Blackstaff Press, *Art in Ulster 2: 1957-77:* Mike Catto; Blackstaff Press.

Fiction:

Ronan Bennett: *The Catastropist;* Headline.
Eamonn Sweeney: *Waiting for the Healer;* Picador.
Lana Citron: *Sucker;* Secker and Warburg.

Non-fiction:

Edna Longley: *The Living Stream;* Bloodaxe.
Sean O'Brien: *The Deregulated Muse;* Bloodaxe.
Eavan Boland: *Object Lessons;* Vintage.
Neil Corcoran: *The Poetry of Seamus Heaney;* Faber.
Gerald Dawe: *The Rest is History;* Abbey Press.
Nature in Ireland: A Scientific and Cultural History: ed John Wilson Foster; Lilliput.
Tim Robinson: *Setting Foot on the Shores of Connemara;* Lilliput.
E Estyn Evans: *Ireland and the Atlantic Heritage;* Lilliput.
R B McDowell: *Crisis & Decline: The Fate of Southern Unionists;* Lilliput.

Poetry:

Jean O'Brien: *The Shadow Keeper;* Salmon.
Tony Curtis: *3 Songs of Home;* Dedalus.
Odes to the Future: Offered to Pearse Hutchinson.
Sean Dunne; *Time and the Island;* Gallery.
Frank Ormsby: *The Ghost Train;* Gallery.

Robert Welch: *Secret Societies;* Dedalus.
Francis Harvey: *The Boa Island Janus;* Dedalus.
Gerard Beirne: *Digging my Own Grave;* Dedalus.
Colm Brennan: *Pitchap and Pike;* Dedalus.
Katherine Duffy: *The Erratic Behaviour of Tides;* Dedalus.
Michael O'Dea: *Sunfire;* Dedalus.
Patrick R Ryan: *Ballad and Balance;* Halcyon Press.
Chris Agee; *In the New Hampshire Woods;* Dedalus.

Drama:

Jennifer Johnston: *The Nightingale and Not the Lark;* Raven Arts.

Also Received:

Thomas Transtromer/ Robin Fulton: *The Sorrow Gondola;* Dedalus.
Ernst Jandl/ Michael Hamburger: *Dingfest/ Thingsure;* Dedalus.
Katie Donovan: *Entering the Mare;* Bloodaxe.
Marvin Bell: *Wednesday: Selected Poems 1966-77;* Salmon.
Gwyn Parry: *Crossings;* Salmon.
Cultural Traditions in Northern Ireland: eds John Erskine & Gordon Lucy; Institute of Irish Studies.
A Fistful of Pens: eds Seamus Keenan & Paul Laughlin.
Signals: ed Adrian Rice; Abbey Press.
W P Journal: Literature and Arts Bimonthly: ed Simion D.
Argus: ed Simion D; Millennium Three Press.
Poetry of the Second World War: ed Desmond Graham; Pimlico.
Scar on the Stone: Poetry from Bosnia: ed Chris Agee; Bloodaxe.
The Leonard L Milbee Collection of Irish Poetry: Compiled by J Howard Woolmer; Princeton Uni Library.

Magazines

Agenda: ed Patricia McCarthy; Irish Poetry Double Issue; *Poetry Ireland; Cyphers.*

Pamphleteer

"I don't want to be too hard on our superiors, but I think frankly that of what is interesting in the lust (last), say twenty years of Scottish writing, I have written it all," said Alexander Trocchi at The Edinburgh Writers' Conference in 1962, his response to Hugh MacDiarmid's infamous "cosmopolitan scum" jibe. More of Mr MacDiarmid later. Whether or not you agree with Scotland's later literary outlaw, one thing that's certain is that through re-issuing of his books, largely from Rebel Inc, Trocchi, some fourteen years after his death, looks finally to have lost his mantle as the forgotten man of Scottish letters. Gavin Bowd's superb essay, *The Outsiders' Alexander Trocchi and Kenneth White* published by Akros, £3.95, is further testament to the resurrection of 'underground' or 'exiled' writers returning to the 'mainstream'.

Of the dozen or so books under the microscope this issue, perhaps the two most significant are from Latin America. White Adder Press have published Jose Watanabe's third collection of poetry, *Path Through the Canefields* (translated by C A De Lomellni and David Tipton). Arguably the most important poet to emerge from South America in recent years Watanabe writes:

The iguana is a real animal, though mythical.
The old man decapitates it
and its blood drips into an earthware pot
and the dog licks the glutinous red stuff as if it
were addicted

Chilean born performance poet Ricardo Corvalan's first solo collection *The Language of Rain*, published by Chilli Pepper Press, with an introduction by Benjamin Zephaniah, is a quirky, upbeat-offering which blends politics, fruit and veg and sex with a spiritual eye.

Next up is a selection of Scottish Poetry also published by Akros. Lillias Forbes' *Turning a Fresh Eye* (£3.75) is a selection of poetry composed since the publication of *Poems of Love*. The aforesaid Hugh MacDiarmid evidently more an admirer of Forbes that Trocchi wrote: "This purity, the impulses of our own hearts; an utterance uncontaminated by merely literary fashions – these are

the virtues of her verse . . . What all this amounts to is simple integrity". *Scottish Selection: Poems* by Tessa Ransford (Akros, £2.45) is a selection from her eight previous collections, released to celebrate her sixtieth birthday. Similarly, Maurice Lindsay's *Speaking Likenesses*, from Scottish Cultural Press, is a celebratory volume of poetry to mark the poet's eightieth birthday. In his latest postscript, Lindsay looks to have lost none of his celebrated charms.

> Sometimes in the morning
> the sun wakes discretely
> from the edge of the earth
> in uprising and sweetly
> contends with the dark
> which disperses completely
> to start the day
> on Blue Mountain.

writes Fred Andrew in 'Over Blue Mountain' from *Unbound: Selected Poems* printed by Clydeside Press (£2.50).

A Wet Handle by Ivor Culter (ARC publication, £4) is a pocket-sized collection of bland and boring poems. Illustrated not by a four year old as it first appears but by the author himself. Immature and too cute by half. On a brighter note, *The Green Crayon Man* by William Oxley, his ninth collection of shorter poems, displays the depth and fragility of a master-craftsman at play (Rockingham Press, £6.96). *The Impending Desert – Poetry or Prose?* by Glasgow born author Joanne Middleton (published by New Millenium, £4.95), explores eco-issues and their effects on future generations. This collection split, into four sections; Topical, A View of North Berwick, Sons and Daughters and Reminiscences, displays the inconsistent flaws of an yet to find her voice. 'Poetry or Prose?' – evidently a question Middleton must herself address.

Fidelities III is a selection of poetry by writers of Pietermaritzburg, an unbalanced offering which all too often disappoints, rarely shines and seldom satisfies. The Rafter Press have issued a limited edition of 50 copies of *Triggerpoints* – poems by Rennie Hirschon, Gillian Stone and Jenyth Worsley. The poems in this collection were read at Kicking Daffodils II, a celebration of women's poetry held at Oxford Brookes University in 1997. Indian born poet Geet Thayil's *Apocalypso* (AARK ARTS) is a beautiful selection of verse, well structured and rich in rhyme. In 'Apocalypse Angels' Thayil writes:

In America the angels rot young,
their cheeks are hollow
blowing out forest fires.
They carry marks of past beauty
on earlobe, nipple, bicep, nostril.

What makes Thayil rhymes most interesting is their honest, their irreverence and their innocent beauty.

Last, yet certainly not least we have the pleasure and melancholy madness of Ruth Padel, a writer of some substance and verve. In this, her fourth collection of poetry, *Rembrandt Would have Loved You* (Chatto Poetry, £7.99) Padel displays the confidence of a writer in full flight. . . . both lyrical and highly charged. Rembrandt may have indeed loved this.

Whatever self is, I'd like mine to wake up with y
yours
While sleep is still plumping the skin,
Warm bread rising in the oven,
An enamel oven, opened on a summer morning
In a village in Provence.

Gary Flockhart

Catalogue

Quite a few books in this section would certainly have deserved a 'proper' review. One of them is *The Faber Book of War Poetry* edited by Kenneth Baker (Faber, £11.99). This anthology intends to give an overview of how poets have responded to the subject of war in different centuries and countries; the main focus however is on Britain. The book includes poems about all sides of the war, the suffering and horrors as well as heroism, comradeship and the nature of bravery. Apart from well-known poets from Homer to Shakespeare, Kipling and e e cummings there are numerous poems by 'ordinary' men and women who recorded their very personal experiences with war. Unfortunately, publi-

cation dates of the individual poems and their sources are missing.

Another book which aims at analysing the multiple meanings of war is Gill Plain's *Women's Fiction of the Second World War: Gender, Power and Resistance* (Edinburgh University Press). Plain endeavours not to define the 'reality of the war' but to explore the literary responses to those realities. Analysing the work of Elizabeth Bowen, Naomi Mitchison, Dorothy L Sayers, Stevie Smith and Virginia Woolf, her central question is how women think about, write about, and, crucially, survive the cultural, emotional and physical dislocations of the Second World War, given that society has long constructed women in opposition to war. Some knowledge of feminist literary theory, especially French feminist theory, is therefore certainly helpful for reading this learnéd and well-written study. The comprehensive introduction gives some background information and sets up a frame for the literary analyses which are not only interesting from the specific angle of the treatment of war.

Even though the book marks the Oxford don's 80th birthday, *The Literary Essays of John Heath-Stubbs*, edited by A T Tolley (Carcanet, £14.95), is certainly not 'academically over the top'. Heath-Stubbs's essays from 1945 to 1989, mainly on poets from the Augustan and Romantic Ages, are very readable and display his intimate knowledge of the poets and their work as well as his involvement with literary tradition.

Chatto & Windus's 1997 edition of Norman MacCaig's *Selected Poems* (£8.99) contains some of his best poetry from 1955 until 1988 and six previously unpublished poems, largely from his last years of writing. Together with Douglas Dunn's introduction this certainly is a treasure for both connoisseurs and for those approaching the work of this Scottish icon for the first time.

Carcanet has published three new volumes of poetry by Jorie Graham (*The Errancy*, £9.95), Peter Bland (*Selected Poems*, £9.95) and Neil Powell (*Selected Poems*, £8.95). Besides these, there is a new edition of H D's famous war *Trilogy* brought together for the first time by Carcanet in 1973 (£8.95). From the same stable comes *Enigmas & Arrivals* (£9.95). This anthology of Commonwealth Writing marks ten years of the Commonwealth Writers Prize, assembling short stories, extracts from longer works of fiction and some poetry from winners of the prize over the last ten years. The book introduces readers to lesser-known writers and the rich variety of 'the new literatures' as well as providing works from best-selling authors such as Mordecai Richler and Vikram Seth.

Another anthology, based on the 1996 Sandbury-Livesay Anthology Contest, has been published by UnMon America under the title *Doors of the Morning*. It collects winning poems by Colin Mackay, Jim C Wilson, Elise McKay and others. This book is meant as a start to an annual series of anthologies which will celebrate the non-elitist 'Populist Poetry' or 'People's Poetry'.

Concerning Scotland there are new books worth noticing in both the literary, socio-cultural and historical fields. Contemporary Scottish poetry is now available to speakers of Italian thanks to the translations of Andrea Fabbri, Walter Morani and Paolo Severini; *Seguendo La Traccia: Poesia scozzese contemporanea*; published by Mobydick.

Thanks to Luath Press we now have the first accessible edition of *Blind Harry's Wallace* in verse form since 1859. Originally produced by William Hamilton of Gilbertfield in 1722, both the novel and the film *Braveheart* are based on this version. The volume conveys the pace and the essence of the original and is surprisingly easy to read. Elspeth King's thorough introduction, explanations of Scots words no longer in general use as well as Owain Kirby's illustrations turn this so far unavailable work into a fascinating and enjoyable reading experience – and it's affordable to everyone at £7.50. Also by Luath Press is Magnus Magnusson's (natural) history of the Hebridean island of Rum (*Rum: Nature's Island*, £7.95), which tells you all about the people, the history, the flora and fauna of this island . . . it makes you want to go there and see it all! Francis Thompson's *The Supernatural Highlands* by the same publisher (£8.99), takes a closer look at witchcraft, ghosts, fairies and other supernatural phenomena which so often are simply dismissed as superstition. Also a vivid account of rural life in the Highlands it underlines the significance of traditional heritage and folk tradition.

This is also true of Robert Smith's book *Land of the Lost* (John Donald, £9.95), which explores the lost settlements in the north-east of Scotland that were deserted in the late 18th century due to famine, poverty and army recruiting. It tells the story of the old crofting communities, trying to trace the life in the old days and a sense of the past. Bridget Mackenzie's *Piping Traditions of the North of Scotland* (John Donald, £20) is mainly intended as a guide and reference work for pipers and piping enthusiasts; however, it may also appeal to music lovers, tourists or historians. The volume collects research by the author herself and by some of her colleagues and covers in detail just about every aspect of piping in the north of Scotland: the piping families, the traditions, the music, the composers, the competitions, the bands, the teachers and so on. For the specialist as well as for the general reader is *The Archaeology of Argyll* edited by Graham Ritchie (Edinburgh Uni Press, £17.95). It contains articles by experts on topics such as early settlements, prehistoric rock carvings and early Christian archaeology. Many helpful illustrations add to the vividness of the volume.

Designed for tourists but certainly also useful for residents is the fourth edition of Peter Irvine's guide *Scotland the Best* (Harper Collins, £9.99). It is basically a handbook of information about all the 'best' places in Scotland: accommodation, food and drink, outdoor places and activities, historical places etc. There are maps and an index to help you find these without difficulties. The second volume of James U Thomson's *Edinburgh Curiosities* (John Donald, £7.95) is a challenge even to natives of the city. It is a different history of Edinburgh, concentrating on the lesser-known but often exciting and amusing details of Edinburgh life such as a murdered policeman on Hogmanay or two Leith men inventing the Christmas card. There are 100 quiz questions at the end to test your knowledge and memory.

There are two reprints of picture guides to Shetland and Orkney (The Shetland Times, both £4.95). They assemble some of the best pictures of the fascinating landscape in all seasons from picture calendars – so it's a must for all Shetland- and Orkney-lovers. Shetland is also the focus of two language books by the same publisher. *The Shetland Dictionary* by John J Graham (£9.95) is a revised version of the 1979 edition, containing over 300 more words. Example sentences and explanations of the meaning and word usage turn this book into more than a simple dictionary. T A Robertson's and John J Graham's *Grammar and Usage of the Shetland Dialect* (£6.95) is a good introduction to this neglected dialect. It has sections on all aspects of grammar and always gives examples from literature and colloquial speech, which makes the book more accessible for home learners. Scots with all its regional variations still needs succour. Scottish Cultural Press is doing its share by publishing a sequel to *Teach Yourself Doric*, which is intended for the more advanced student: *Doric for Swots* by Douglas Kynoch (£4.95). From the same publisher comes *Doric Proverbs & Sayings* (ed by Douglas Kynoch also £4.95). This collection is formed from two older collections by Helen Beaton and Alexander Fenton plus some items from other books in Doric and is a treasury for those who know Doric as well as for those who want to learn it.

Ute Meiners

Notes on Contributors

Chris Agee: Former editor of *Poetry Ireland Review* and has edited *Scar on Stone: Contemporary Poetry from Bosnia* (Bloodaxe). He is completeing a new poetry collection, *First Light*.

Ernest Bates lives in Ireland after nearly 40 years in exile. He is married to the painter Daphne Plessner. A selection of poems will be published next spring.

John Behan: Born in 1938 in Dublin. Internationally renowned artist/sculptor. Works from studio in Galway.

Eavan Boland: Born Dublin 1944. *Collected Poems* (1995), *The Lost Land* (1998). Lecturer at Stanford University, California.

Eva Bourke originally from Germany, has lived in Galway for over 20 years. Has written 3 poetry collections and 2 anthologies of Irish poetry in German translation.

Paddy Bushe born in Dublin in 1948 and now lives in Co Kerry. He has published three collections of poems, including *To Make a Stone Sing*, a collaboration with the painter Catriona O'Connor.

Peter Cameron: brought up in Newton-grange where Scots is used everyday and daily, left school at 15. He is a reader in a small printing firm outside Edinburgh. Has been published in *Lallans*. Retires in 3 years.

Colette Connor: poet/playwright. Short-listed for a Hennessy Award 1994. Published *Poetry Ireland Review, HU, Books Ireland*, etc.

John F Deane: born Achhill Island, 1943; founded Poetry Ireland and *The Poetry Ireland Review*. Latest collection *Christ, with Urban Fox*. Won the O'Shaughnessy Award for Irish Poetry 1998.

Patrick Deeley has published 3 collections of poems including *Turane: The Hidden Village*. His fourth *Succession of Canopies* is due from Dedalus Press in Spring 2000.

Francis Devine, born London 1949, is a trade union tutor in Dublin. He was joint editor of *Saothar: Journal of the Irish Labour History Society*. His first collection is *Red Star, Blue Moon* (Elo Publications, 1997).

Gerard Donovan: born in Wexford, Ireland. He has written two books of poems: *Columbus Rides Again* and *Kings and Bicycles*.

Nancy Doyle: born in New York City in 1929. Has lived in Dublin since 1965. Has had poems published in Ireland, England and USA – these are the first to be published in Scotland.

Eibhlín Evans teaches at Hertfordshire University, specialising in modernist and contemporary poetry. She has published work on Anglo-Irish writing and on women's poetry.

Peter Fallon edits and publishes Gallery Books in Co Meath. *News of the World: Selected and New Poems* appeared this year.

Gabriel Fitzmaurice: Prolific poet, translator and editor. Director of the Listowel Writers Conference in Co Kerry where he lives.

Patrick Galvin: Born in Cork, Ireland – his books include *Christ in London* (1960) and *New and Selected Poems*, Cork University Press 1996.

Robert Greacen: born in Derry in 1920. His *Collected Poems* won the 1995 *Irish Times* Poetry Award. His recent collection is *Protestant Without a Horse*.

Rody Gorman: Born in Dublin 1960. His collection *Fax and Other Poems* was published by Polygon in 1996.

Vona Groarke's first collection is *Shale* (Gallery Press, 1994), poems from which are included in Bloodaxe's *Making for Planet Alice*. Her second collection *Other's People's Houses* is due in early 1999.

Michael Hartnett: Born 1941 in Limerick, based in Dublin. His eagerly awaited book of translations of O Rathaille is forthcoming from The Gallery Press.

Seamus Heaney has recently published *Opened Ground*, a selection from all his volumes of poems from 1966-1996

Seán Hutton has published four collections of poems of which *Seachrán Ruairí* was awarded the Seán Ó Ríordáin prize.

Pearse Hutchinson: Born 1927 in Glasgow, based in Dublin. Writes in Gaelic and English and has translated from Catalan and Galician.

Fred Johnston has published six collections of poetry, one novel and a collection of short stories, *Keeping the Night Watch*. He founded Galway's annual literature festival, CUIRT.

Brendan Kennelly has written several

books of verse, two novels, four plays and a collection of essays. He teaches English at Trinity College, Dublin.

Kevin Kiely has published two novels, his most recent *Mere Mortals,* written a radio play *Multiple Indiscretions* and has had poetry published in various journals.

Thomas Kinsella: Born 1928. Translations from the Irish: *The Tain,* 1969; *Poems of the Dispossessed,* 1981. Editor of the *New Oxford Book of Irish Verse,* with all new translations. Recent publications: *Collected Poems,* OUP 1986 and *The Pen Shop,* Peppercanister, 1997.

Alan Long is currently taking a year out after finishing high school, and he hopes to study Journalism at college. The printing of 'Thirteen' is his first real break.

Michael Longley: Born 1939 in Belfast. *Gorse Fires* (1991) won the Whitbread Prize for Poetry. Has just published his *Selected Poems.*

Bernard MacLaverty born Belfast. In 1975 moved to Scotland and now lives in Glasgow. *Grace Notes,* his latest book, won the Saltire Scottish Book of the Year (1997).

Hugh Maxton: Born 1947 in Wicklow. Real name William John MacCormac. Head of the Dept of English, Goldsmith College, where he holds the chair of Literary History.

Ute Meiners is a student at the University of Göettingen in Germany. She was a volunteer at Chapman over the summer.

Dan Mulhall, Ireland's first Consul General to Scotland, took up his post in 1998. His previous diplomatic postings were in India, Austria and Belgium. His first book, *Ireland at the Turn of the Century,* is due out in March.

Art Murphy: Newry poet, widely published: *Poetry Ireland Review, Incognito, New Welsh Review, Understanding, Connections.*

Hayden Murphy: Born 1945 in Dublin. Poet and Arts journalist based in Edinburgh. Editor of the unique literary broadsheet *Broadsheet* (much missed in Sandy Bells).

Jean O'Brien was born and works in Dublin. She is a founding member of the Dublin Writers' Workshop. Her collection *The Shadow Keeper* was published by Salmon in 1997.

Conor O'Callaghan's first collection *The History of Rain* (Gallery Press, 1993) was short-listed for the Forward Best First Collection

Prize. *Seatown* will appear in early 1999.

Ciaran O'Driscoll lives in Limerick. He has published four collection of poetry, the most recent *The Old Women of Magione* (Dedalus).

Desmond O'Grady was born in Limerick and has written 16 collections of poetry, including *The Road Taken 1956-1996* and 10 of translated poetry, including *Trawling Tradition, 1954-1994* and prose memoirs.

Eugene O'Sullivan: Not born but created. Often known as 'Anon'.

Adrian Rice is a Belfast poet and the editor of Abbey Press. Author of *Muck Island* and *Impediments,* his first full collection, *The Mason's Tongue,* is due in 1999.

Mark Roper's latest chapbook is *The Home Fire* (Abbey Press). Other collections include *The Hen Ark* (Peterloo/Salmon, 1990) and *Catching the Light* (Peterloo/Lagan, 1997).

Rosemarie Rowley works include *Flight into Reality* (Rowan Tree Press 1989) and *Electric Shock Treatment and Sylvia Plath's Life and Work* (Thumbscrew). Her latest collection of poetry is *The Wake of Wonder* .

Peter Sirr's most recent collection is *The Ledger of Fruitful Exchange* (Gallery Press). He is an editor of *Graph*: Irish Cultural review and Director of the Irish Writers' Centre.

Eithne Strong: born in Limerick in 1923. She is a writer in English and Irish, poetry, fiction. She has ten books to date, the most recent in English *Spatial Nosing* and *Nobel* (1998).

Eleanor Thomson: lecturer, born Glasgow. Short stories, poetry and articles published in various magazines and newspapers. Wishes she could write full time.

Suzanne Thomson, once resident of St Andrews and Edinburgh, lives in Oklahoma, producing fiction on many levels and is much too deeply involved in theatre.

Macdara Woods: Born in Dublin 1942. Six collections of poetry; his *Selected Poems* appeared in 1996. Founding-editor of literary magazine *Cyphers,* 1975; 2 volumes of poetry in translations scheduled, Italy late 1998.